PAMELLA Z. ASQUITH'S
FRUIT TART COOKBOOK

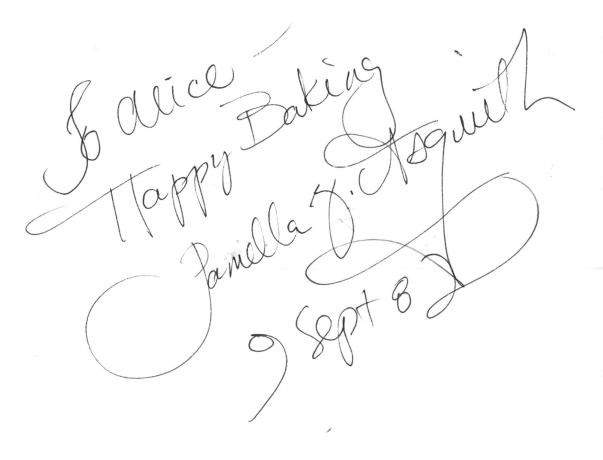

To alice
Happy Baking
Pamella Z. Asquith

9 Sept 8

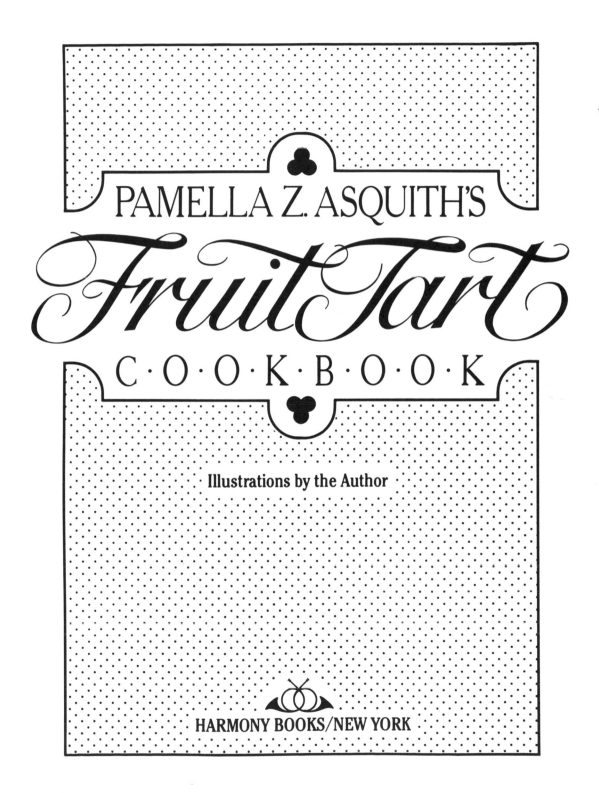

PAMELLA Z. ASQUITH'S

Fruit Tart

C·O·O·K·B·O·O·K

Illustrations by the Author

HARMONY BOOKS/NEW YORK

Designed by Ken Sansone

Published by Harmony Books, a division of Crown Publishers, Inc., One Park Avenue, New York, New York 10016, and simultaneously in Canada by General Publishing, Ltd. HARMONY BOOKS and colophon are trademarks of Crown Publishers, Inc.

Manufactured in the United States of America

Library of Congress Cataloging in Publication Data
Asquith, Pamella Z.
    Pamella Z. Asquith's Fruit tart cookbook.

    Includes index.
    1. Pastry.   2. Cookery (Fruit)   I. Title.
II. Title: Fruit tart cookbook.
TX773.A86   641.8'652   81-23773
ISBN 0-517-54621-3   AACR2

10 9 8 7 6 5 4 3 2 1
First Edition

ACKNOWLEDGMENTS

I gratefully acknowledge the help of the following people: Robert Cooperstein for his multifaceted support; Joyce Cole, my indefatigable agent; Judy Knipe, Madame Lili LeCocq; the YCC Camp, Mount Diablo, California, 1980, which put up with my usurping the staff typewriter when I should have been cooking for them; the two-year-old fruit tart enthusiast, Beau Cronin, who became very excited whenever he saw a flat white box because he thought it contained a fruit tart for him; his father, Isaac Cronin; my generous and critical photographer, Marshall Berman; and my editor, Harriet Bell.

CONTENTS

INTRODUCTION

I set out on the path of life with absolutely no intention of becoming a professional pastry chef. Cooking and baking had been only a minor hobby for me, because my mother approached cooking with such disdain. (No, I cannot boast of a French grandmother whose secrets I am passing on; I have absolutely no Gallic blood, and my mother and grandmother both hated cooking.) While in college, needing part-time employment, and fancying myself a good bread baker, I got a job in a French bakery. After college, I soon realized that there were more opportunities for professional chefs than for art historians (my field), and I have been cooking and making pastry ever since. I do approach cooking and baking as an art form, pastry in particular offering means for creative expression. If I had to choose my favorite area of pastry making, it would be fruit tarts, both for the beauty of the object and the pleasure of the making.

The open-face, single-crust fruit tart is part of many national cuisines. In Spain, it is called *flan;* in France, *tarte;* in Sweden, *tarta;* in England, *tart.* In the United States, there is still some confusion between a tart and a pie, but in Berkeley, my home, the only people who refer to tarts as pies are transplanted French people, who pronounce it as two syllables, "pi-e."

Basically, the difference between a pie and a tart is that a pie is usually baked with a fruit filling (prepared with plenty of sugar); a tart is made with uncooked or poached fruit, and is not as sweet. Pies may feature fruit fillings, but a tart features the fruit itself.

Fruit tarts must be assembled at the last minute for perfection of texture and subtlety of flavor. With such evanescent quality, they truly

9

need to be homemade, and so are an exceptionally rewarding subject for a cookbook. Even a fruit tart purchased at the finest bakery may be past its moment of sublimity by serving time. If all the components of a tart are on hand, it can be assembled within three minutes. With this book, you need never again endure a soggy crust or tasteless fruit overexposed to oxygen.

Tartes aux fruits are as ubiquitous in France as ice cream is in the United States; they are simply taken for granted. Every French person is virtually born with a favorite recipe for *pâte demi-feuilletée* (flaky pastry dough) and *crème pâtissière* (pastry cream). *Tartes aux fruits? Récréation d'enfant!* (Child's play!)

Although fruit tarts have become quite popular in metropolitan communities on the East and West Coasts, they are largely unknown elsewhere in the United States. Perhaps someday people in this country will be so accustomed to fruit tarts that a book such as this will no longer be necessary. In the meantime, let this book introduce the fruit tart to cooks all across the United States, and perhaps its legacy will become part of this country's culinary tradition.

The art of making fruit tarts, like that of playing Mozart piano sonatas or making Japanese flower arrangements, is deceptively simple. The would-be fruit tart artist need not be intimidated. Only a few basic techniques, such as rolling a pastry tart shell, or cooking a pastry cream or glaze to its moment of perfection, need be mastered, and, of course, you can always eat your mistakes. (I know of at least three cats that are lumpy-pastry-cream enthusiasts!) There is no substitute for experience when it comes to rolling a pastry tart shell; however, there is also no substitute for that mysterious innate "touch" that makes a great pastry chef. (If you have low blood pressure, and thus cool hands, you may consider yourself blessed.) During my years in the profession, I knew of several excellent chefs who would feign apoplexy at the suggestion that they make a pastry tart shell, or even touch yeast.

Before you attempt your first fruit tart, carefully read the chapters on "Ingredients" and "Equipment." They contain elaborations, hints and tips not found in the individual recipes. Finally, when the moment of arranging the fruit on the pastry base comes, remember the Mozart sonata—each piece of fruit should follow another as if it were inevitable and there could be no other way for the slices to fall.

Ingredients

Ingredients

When making fruit tarts, always remember that parsimony does not pay! By making a tart yourself, you are already saving a lot of money. To get a better idea of how cheap a homemade fruit tart really is, multiply your savings by two to take into account the increase in quality of your homemade tart over a store-bought one. It is silly to skimp on ingredients. As one French chef I knew put it, "You start with good stuff, you get good stuff. Start with junk, you get junk." Don't fool yourself—stale eggs, old cream or fruit before or past its prime will all affect the taste of a tart, whose beauty is in its simplicity and subtlety.

BUTTER

Purchase only fresh, unadulterated butter. The recipes in this book specify unsalted (sweet) butter, since the subtleties of fruit can easily be overpowered by an overabundance of salt. Butter can be stored in the freezer.

CREAM, MILK, SOUR CREAM AND CREAM CHEESE

Buy only fresh, unadulterated dairy products. Avoid "ultrapasteurized" snow-white cream; it is full of vegetable gums, which may react to cooking in undesirable ways. Health food stores are a reliable place to shop for high-quality unadulterated dairy products. Buy cream cheese with no salt or vegetable gums, if possible.

EGGS

The recipes call for eggs graded large. They should be as fresh as possible. A stale egg will float when put in water.

FLOUR

Using the proper flour for pastry is crucial. It must be fresh, but it need not be bleached. Flour is classified according to how much protein it contains. Wheat grown in cooler climates or in cool seasons tends to be rich in protein, and is called "strong." Wheat grown in warmer places and seasons has more starch, and is called "weak." Flour for pastry is a combination of these strong and weak types and should contain approximately 8 percent protein. All-purpose flour has 11 percent protein, and cake flour has 7 percent protein. Therefore, you can make your own pastry flour by mixing these two readily available flours, 60 percent cake flour to 40 percent all-purpose. Do this by weight, not volume; the two flours have different weights per volume. Some health food stores carry special flours, or perhaps your local bakery will sell you some pastry flour (be sure to go in at a slow time and ask *very* nicely). See the Mail Order Guide on page 133 if it is impossible to obtain pastry flour in your area. Three recipes in this book require pastry flour: Classic Puff Pastry Tart Shell, Flaky Pastry Tart Shell and Whole Wheat Flaky Pastry Tart Shell. The other recipes use all-purpose flour.

Store flour in a cool, dry place or well sealed in the freezer. Flour *must* be sifted before measuring if you are to get an accurate measurement by volume. Sift it onto a plate, then spoon it into the measuring cup (do *not* pack the flour into the cup) and level the cup with a knife. Personally, I think this method is absurd, and I always measure flour by weight. Buy a scale—you will never regret it. Most people I know are incredibly conservative regarding measuring, but once they have overcome the inertia and changed from one system of measurement to another, they are grateful.

FLAVORINGS AND SPICES

The use of flavoring extracts is discouraged; there is no such thing as a pure extract. I recommend that you make your own vanilla sugar (page 18) instead of using vanilla extract. The methods of extraction employ a wide range of chemicals (including what is commonly known as automotive antifreeze), which inevitably affect the taste. If you're to go to all the trouble to make a classical *crème pâtissière,* why pollute it with flavoring extracts?

Unground spices will keep their flavors for years, but as soon as they are ground they oxidize and become no more useful than sawdust. Spices should be purchased whole and stored away from heat in dry, airtight, opaque containers.

If whole spices or vanilla beans are not available in your area, consult the Mail Order Guide (page 133).

FRUIT

Ideally, fruit should be eaten within hours of being picked, but that is almost impossible these days. Therefore, do not purchase fruit too far ahead of time. Generally a fleshy fruit's ripeness can be judged by touch. Fruit goes through four stages: hard (completely underripe), firm (slightly underripe), soft (ripe) and mushy (overripe). Allow your eyes and nose to judge when a fruit is ripe, also; the colors and smells should be intense.

Apples should be firm and free of bruises or brown spots. Store apples at a cool room temperature, not necessarily under refrigeration. Tart apples, such as Pippins, Gravenstein or Granny Smith, are the best for baking.

Apricots may be bought slightly underripe; they will become soft when baked. Look out for brown spots and bruises. Refrigerate fully ripe apricots; store underripe apricots at room temperature.

Banana ripening has been perfected by retailers, so it is usually possible to buy good bananas. If the only bananas you can find are green, however, allow them to sit at room temperature a day or two until they become yellow. Never refrigerate bananas.

Berries are very difficult to store and can be underripe and moldy at the same time. Berries do ripen if allowed to sit at room temperature, but if any moisture gets on them, or if a berry is crushed and exudes moisture, mold will grow immediately. To be safe, buy only berries that are ripe and ready to be eaten; do not store them. Fresh blackberries, blueberries, olallieberries and raspberries (not strawberries) can be frozen without too great a sacrifice to their taste and texture. Do not wash; wrap very well in plastic bags and squeeze out any air pockets.

Cherries are ripe if they are a deep, rich color and are sweet, not tart. Cherries will ripen if allowed to sit at room temperature; refrigerate ripe cherries, rinsed and dried, pitted, well-wrapped with no air pockets. Fresh cherries can be frozen.

Cranberries are usually sold only fully ripe. Cranberries do not lose taste or texture when frozen.

Currants and grapes should be eaten immediately after being picked; time spent off the vine does not improve them. Refrigerate until serving time.

Citrus growers have perfected ripening of their products, so usually grapefruit, oranges, lemons, limes and tangerines are ready to be eaten when purchased.

Kiwi fruit should be soft but not mushy. An underripe kiwi will turn your mouth inside out when you bite into it. Kiwis will ripen if allowed to sit at room temperature a day or two. Refrigerate ripe kiwis.

Loquats (page 104) should be soft and bright yellow. Do not pick them until they are ready (I am assuming that anyone who will make this tart has a loquat tree in their yard as, fortunately, I do).

Mangoes and papayas are soft, not mushy, when ripe and should be free of brown spots and bruises. Mangoes and papayas will ripen if allowed to sit at room temperature. Refrigerate the ripe fruit.

Nectarines, peaches and pears to be poached should be slightly underripe. They will ripen if allowed to sit at room temperature; if ripe, refrigerate them. D'Anjou pears are the best variety for poaching.

Persimmons should be soft, intense of color and free of brown spots or bruises. Like an underripe kiwi fruit, an underripe persimmon is nothing to serve an honored guest.

Pineapples are golden, not green, when ripe. A leaf in the middle of the crown of the pineapple will pull out easily if the pineapple is ripe. Pineapples will ripen if allowed to sit at room temperature. Refrigerate ripe pineapples.

Plums to be baked may be slightly underripe, but plums to be used uncooked should be soft. Plums will ripen if allowed to sit at room temperature; if ripe, refrigerate them.

Quinces, even when ripe, will be very hard. Poaching is necessary to make them palatable.

Rhubarb should be firm (like celery) and pink.

USING FRESH FRUIT Fruit that will be peeled does not have to be washed. Rinse other fruit thoroughly with cool water and gently rub dry or allow it to drain dry. Berries purchased already stemmed need not necessarily be washed; indeed, washing them could leach out a lot of flavor. Wash stemmed berries only if they are dirty or dusty.

To cut or slice fruit, always use a very sharp knife, preferably stainless steel (see page 23). Follow the instructions in each recipe for cutting and slicing fruit. In general, lay the fruit to be sliced flat on the

cutting surface; hold the knife in one hand while anchoring the fruit with the other hand; slice slightly away from your fingers at an angle of about 105°; with every slice, move your fingers down the fruit. With a little practice you should be able to do this evenly and very quickly.

Excessively juicy fruit such as poached fruit or pineapple should be drained before being placed on a tart lest it make the crust soggy immediately. Lay the fruit segments on a cloth or paper towel for a few minutes to absorb excess moisture.

Certain fruits such as peaches, pears and nectarines require poaching to render them more palatable. Follow the instructions in each individual recipe.

Once the fruit is sliced it should be handled as little as possible, to prevent bruising. Arrange fruit segments on the tart with a knife if you feel comfortable handling a knife; otherwise use your fingers.

Certain fruits benefit by being mixed; complementary fruits are indicated in the recipes. Do not get carried away and try to arrange every fruit in season on a tart, or the overall effect will be a sweet pulpy mess. (Not too tutti-frutti, please!)

USING DRIED FRUIT Select only the finest-looking (free from discoloration) and chemically unadulterated dried fruit.

Sulfur, used to dry some fruit, is volatile when exposed to heat. The sulfur leaves a bitter aftertaste and should be leached out. Cover the dried fruit with boiling water. Allow it to steep 2 minutes and then drain off the water. Repeat until the "burned hair" smell is gone.

Dried fruit can be partially rehydrated by marinating. This also adds flavor and makes it easier to chew. Dried fruit can be marinated in either a brandy syrup or a caramel syrup.

To make the brandy syrup, put an equal amount of water and sugar in a heavy saucepan and bring to a boil. Simmer for 5 minutes and cool. Add one third as much brandy and pour over the dried fruit. Cover and allow to steep in a cool place away from light for at least three days, and up to four or five months.

To make the caramel syrup, put a measured amount of sugar in a heavy saucepan. Melt the sugar until it turns a dark golden brown. Handle the hot sugar with extreme caution or you will be severely burned. Immediately pour an equal amount of water over the sugar and then pour this over the fruit. Cover and allow to steep at least three days in a cool, dark place.

Different dried fruits can be combined for taste, texture and color

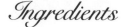

variation. Brown prunes or figs are nicely set off by orange dried apricots, cream-colored dried pears or apples or yellow dried pineapple.

For economy's sake, dry your own fruit when it is cheap and in season. Several devices are commercially available for this procedure. Follow instructions for use.

NUTS

Buy only the freshest nuts. Taste nuts before buying, if possible. A fresh nut will be crunchy, not spongy; a fresh nut will taste almost sweet, not bitter; a fresh nut will be aromatic. Nuts are harvested in autumn, so be wary of nuts sold during the summer months. Walnuts, particularly, due to their high oil content, go rancid if improperly stored by wholesalers.

The flavor of all nuts is enhanced by roasting. To roast them, bake shelled nuts at 375–400°F for 5 to 10 minutes. Shake the baking sheet halfway through the roasting; the nuts nearer the edge of the sheet roast more quickly.

The process of removing the skins from nuts is called blanching. Recipes, such as the Hollandaise Pastry Filling, that require a subtle nut flavor specify blanched nuts. Almonds and hazelnuts are sometimes blanched. To blanch almonds, submerge them in boiling water for 2 minutes, then squeeze the nut through the skin. To blanch hazelnuts, roast them and then rub off the skin (most hazelnuts have a very bitter skin, which should be removed). Store nuts in an airtight container in a cool place. I do not recommend freezing nuts, as this usually affects the taste and texture. Grind nuts just before using; their flavor oils are volatile. Like ancient ground spices, old ground nuts are no more useful than sawdust.

SUGAR

Use granulated white sugar. Store it in an airtight container in a cool place. Many of the recipes in this book call for vanilla sugar. Put a vanilla bean in a well-sealed container of sugar (1–2 pounds). One vanilla bean can flavor many pounds of sugar and is actually cheaper than vanilla extract. Vanilla sugar keeps indefinitely if well sealed.

Equipment

Invest in high-quality equipment; it will last a lifetime (and will probably become heirlooms for your children).

SCALES

Measuring by weight, not volume, is highly recommended. Balance scales remain accurate, unlike many spring scales.

VOLUME MEASURES

Glass or stainless steel measuring cups and bowls are preferable to plastic or aluminum; plastic sometimes affects the taste of foodstuffs, and aluminum may react with fruit acids.

THERMOMETER

A thermometer is not an essential piece of equipment if you trust your judgment. The insecure or inexperienced tart maker is advised to entrust the temperature of a cream to a thermometer that registers to at least 160°F.

SPOONS, CHOPSTICKS AND DOUGH MAKING TOOLS

The simple wooden spoon and humble chopstick are essential tools for the tart maker. Use a chopstick when you want to homogenize ingredients without beating in air, as when melting chocolate or a thick glaze. Avoid plastic or aluminum spoons.

Of all the gadgets marketed under the name of "pastry blenders," nothing works so well as a common table fork or your own hands. When I mix something "by hand," I do so literally. Dig in; your hands are your best tool. Some electric mixers have paddles designed specifically for pastry making.

Weight/Volume Equivalents

Butter 1 cup = 8 ounces

Chocolate, grated 1 cup = 3 ounces

Cocoa 1 tablespoon packed = ¼ ounce
  1 tablespoon sifted and then measured = ⅓ ounce

Coconut, grated 1 cup = 3 ounces
  1 cup packed = 4 ounces

Eggs, whole 1 cup = 4–5
  whites 1 cup = 8–9
  yolks 1 cup = 12–13

Flour or cornstarch 1 cup sifted and then measured = 4 ounces

Honey, liquid 1 cup = 12 ounces

Liquid (water, coffee, liqueur) 1 cup = 8 ounces

Nuts, unblanched, finely ground 1 cup = 4 ounces
  unblanched, finely ground 1 cup packed = 6 ounces
  blanched, finely ground 1 cup packed = 8 ounces

Sugar, powdered or confectioner's 1 cup sifted and then measured =
  4 ounces
  granulated 1 cup = 8 ounces
  brown 1 cup packed = 8 ounces

For all ingredients, for purposes of simplicity, when 1 cup =
8 ounces then ⅓ cup = 2½ ounces and ⅔ cup = 5½ ounces

SPATULAS AND SCRAPERS

Spatulas and scrapers are available in metal, plastic and rubber. To clean a pastry board, use a scraper; a wet sponge will only result in a pasty, messy board.

KNIVES AND SHARPENING EQUIPMENT

Non–stainless steel knives, although they keep a sharp edge longer, will corrode and impart a taste to highly acidic fruit such as citrus fruit. Whether a particular fruit responds better to a flat-edged or serrated knife is indicated in each recipe.

Keep your knives sharp with a stone with two grit grades and a piece of jeweler's rouge or carborundum paper. A sharpening steel does not actually sharpen a knife; it merely aligns or hones the edge.

HOW TO SHARPEN A KNIFE Rub each side of the grit stone with a few drops of mineral or machine oil. Put the stone, coarse side up, in a stable position about hip high. To get better leverage, stand up. Hold the knife at a 15° angle and push the blade across the stone. Turn the blade over and pull it down the stone, again at a 15° angle. Repeat at least a dozen times. Turn the stone over to the finer grit side. Repeat the push-and-pull procedure at least a dozen times. Then, holding it again at a 15° angle, make small circles down the blade of the knife on the rouge paper. Turn the knife over and repeat. To finish, make several long sweeps across the paper or down a sharpening steel, turning the blade over each time. *Repeat this last step every time you use the knife.*

ROLL CUTTER

Professionals use a roll cutter to cut puff pastry. It does not drag through the pastry and destroy the layered effect.

CHOPPING AND CUTTING SURFACE

Use a hardwood board such as maple or oak for chopping and cutting. A marble slab was never intended as a cutting surface and will dull a knife instantly.

NUT AND CHOCOLATE GRINDER

A hand-operated grinder is the best solution for grinding nuts and chocolate. Electric equipment certainly performs the task quicker, but never with the same results.

A TART MAKER'S BATTERIE DE CUISINE

- BALANCE SCALE
- SPRING SCALE
- MEASURING SPOONS
- WIRE WHISK
- MEASURING CUP
- WOODEN SPOON
- RUBBER SCRAPER
- THERMOMETER
- CHOPSTICK
- METAL SCRAPER
- RUBBER SPATULA
- PARING KNIVES
- ROLL CUTTER
- SERRATED KNIFE
- CHOPPING KNIFE
- CLEAVER
- MORTAR AND PESTLE
- BOX GRATER
- PEAR CORER
- PEELER
- NUT OR CHOCOLATE GRINDER
- BLENDER
- NUTMEG GRATER
- SIFTER OR STRAINER

DOUBLE-BOILER

·· SAUCEPAN ··

·· ELECTRIC
MIXER
WITH ··
PASTRY
PADDLE

·ELBOW
PALETTE
·KNIFE·

·· STOCKPOT

PALETTE KNIFE ··

HANDLED ROLLING PIN

JELLY
BAG
WITH
STAND

DOWEL ROLLING PIN ··

·· FOOD
PROCESSOR ·

·· BARQUETTE ··
·TINS·

SPRING-FORM
·PAN·

TART-TIN WITH
··REMOVABLE
BOTTOM ··

·· TARTLET
·TINS·

SUGAR
SHAKER

PASTRY BRUSH

·FLAN RING·

·COOLING RACK·

25

ELECTRICAL APPLIANCES

Electric blenders, food processors and grinders have advantages and limitations. For instance, walnuts or chocolate ground by electrical equipment can quickly turn to mush; but a food processor is the ideal tool for making pastry dough. Follow the instructions in each recipe as to which appliance is advisable.

STRAINERS, SIFTERS AND JELLY BAGS

A wire-mesh strainer can double as a sifter, but not as a jelly bag. A jelly bag, which allows only the liquid of a fruit through its pores, is essential for making a clear glaze. Jelly bags are made of nylon, so an old nylon stocking makes a good jelly bag. Cheesecloth will not do because the mesh is too large.

WHISKS

The action of a wire whisk incorporates air into the foodstuff. A good, heavy-duty whisk will last a lifetime. Choose a size and weight that feels comfortable in your hand. It is a good idea to have at least two different size whisks.

DOUBLE BOILER

The double boiler or *bain marie* is an essential piece of equipment for making classical custards. You can substitute a heavy ceramic or stainless steel bowl set in a saucepan. Do not allow any water to splash into the cooking mixture.

SAUCEPANS AND STOCKPOTS

Stainless steel or enameled saucepans and stockpots are preferred for glaze making. Avoid aluminum; it will react with highly acidic fruit, such as citrus fruit, imparting a bitter taste.

WORK SURFACE

Marble is the traditional and best surface for making pastry. Wood is an excellent substitute. Allow at least four times the area of the rolled pastry as a work surface. Put the marble slab in the freezer prior to use, if possible. Use a scraper, not a sponge, to clean a work surface. Occasionally clean a wooden board by mixing a little bleach with water, scrubbing it into the surface and scraping it off.

....

ROLLING PINS

Two types of rolling pins are available: the handleless dowel type and the handled variety. The dowel type allows for more speed. Tart makers from the old country tell of their mothers using a wine bottle as a substitute for a rolling pin.

TART TINS

The term "tart tin" is actually a misnomer; tart tins are not pure tin, but an alloy that is predominantly steel. Heavy, commercial-gauge tart tins are the only kind worth buying. The lighter (in weight and color) tart tins warp when exposed to high temperatures, and scratch and bend easily. Heavy, dark metal absorbs oven heat evenly and therefore bakes evenly. The imported Cordon Bleu brand is consistently excellent (see the Mail Order Guide, page 133). Avoid using soap on tart tins; rub off any stuck pastry with only a little water, if possible. Before using a brand new tart tin, rub it with vegetable oil, bake the oil in and allow the tin to cool. Do this several times; your tarts may stick if you don't. This is called "priming" the tart tin. Your local bakery supply retailer may have a selection of used equipment; it may be a bargain, and will not need to be primed.

Fruit tarts can be made in any shape or size, but for consistency, all the recipes in this book use a 9½-inch tart tin with a removable bottom. The size is based on the diameter of the removable bottom. Pastry shrinks a little when baked, so your resulting tart shell will be closer to 9 inches than 9½ inches. One 9-inch fruit tart will yield six large or eight good-sized servings.

Do not use a pie pan; it is a most inelegant serving dish and there is no way to remove a baked tart shell intact. A springform cake pan or a flan ring placed on a baking sheet can be substituted for a tart tin.

Small tart tins are called tartlet tins and come in a myriad of sizes and shapes. All the recipes in this book are adaptable to six 4-inch-diameter tartlets. Some of the smaller tartlet tins do not have a removable bottom; don't worry, tartlet shells are easy to handle.

OVEN

A convection oven is the best for pastry baking, but since most of us don't own one, a regular oven is fine—with some vigilance. You know the quirks of your oven best. It may be necessary to rotate a tart shell in a regular oven that has "hot spots."

COOLING RACK

A wire cooling rack is necessary for tarts baked with custard; if any of the custard leaks through the crust, the cooled tart will stick to the tart tin and the tart slices won't lift out easily.

PALETTE KNIVES

Professional elbow or straight-bladed decorating palette knives are useful for spreading pastry cream or dislodging a stuck tart shell. They are available in stainless steel and non–stainless steel.

PASTRY BRUSH

A pastry brush made with nylon bristles or with feathers is used for glazing fruit. Clean your pastry brush with bleach water (1 tablespoon bleach to 1 cup of water), not soap.

PEDESTALED REVOLVING CAKE DECORATING STAND

This makes arranging fruit faster and easier, but it is not necessary. A lazy Susan serves the same function.

SUGAR SHAKER

A sugar shaker acts as a strainer and makes it easy to garnish a tart with powdered sugar.

ALCOHOL SPRITZER

A spritzer or atomizer distributes liqueur evenly over a tart. A plant sprayer will serve the same function. Do not store liqueur in a metal spritzer; its taste may be affected, and it may crystallize and clog the spritzer.

SERVING EQUIPMENT

Fruit tarts should be served on a flat plate. A pedestaled plate makes for an elegant setting. A doily underneath the tart sets it off nicely (do not place the doily underneath the tart until it is completely finished). Use a sharp straight-bladed knife to cut fruit tarts. A wedge-shaped flat blunt knife is the proper tool for serving fruit tarts.

Pastry Doughs

P astry is the foundation of any fruit tart. You may be surprised how easy it is to make pastry once you have mastered a few basic techniques, which are thoroughly outlined in the following pages. Remember that making pastry is not like making soup—you cannot just dump everything together and expect the result to be acceptable. Always measure precisely and follow the directions carefully.

For consistency, all the following recipes yield enough for one 9-inch round tart or six 4-inch round tartlets. Do not limit yourself to these shapes, however. After you have mastered the basic techniques, try free-form tart shells made with puff pastry in any whimsical shape, such as a heart, diamond, octagon or tree.

Last, remember that there is nothing worse than a soggy crust. No matter how great your pastry cream and fruit are, a soggy crust will dominate and spoil the tart. Sometimes this is due simply to insufficient baking or baking at too low a temperature. Some people underbake their pastry and end up with a pale crust. Don't be a blond baker! Always be sure your oven is thoroughly preheated.

TEMPERATURE OF INGREDIENTS

The formation of gluten (musclelike protein fibers created by mixing and kneading a dough) must be inhibited in a pastry dough lest it become tough and stringy. Gluten is not readily formed under cold conditions; therefore, all ingredients that go into a pastry dough should be very cold. Butter must be softened only enough to allow the flour and other ingredients to become incorporated into it, about 55–60°F. Water or other liquid should be as cold as possible.

USING A ROLLING PIN

There are two different kinds of rolling pins (as explained on page 27): the handleless dowel type and the kind with handles mounted on a freely turning axle. For home use, the handleless variety affords more sensitivity to the dough and is therefore preferable. A rolling pin with handles is advantageous only when many pounds of a resilient dough are being worked. Although the grip on the two styles differs, certain principles apply to both. Always exert pressure on the rolling pin perpendicular to the dough (90° angle). Roll the dough from the center outward, never back and forth. Roll the dough no more than necessary.

To make a square or rectangle, roll the dough from the center outward to 12 o'clock, 6 o'clock, 3 o'clock and then 9 o'clock. Flap the dough to relax it, as you would flap a beach towel to get rid of excess sand. Allow an inch to spare on each side for the edge and the edge being folded over: thus, an 8 x 8-inch square tart would need a piece of dough 10 x 10 inches; a 6 x 9-inch rectangular tart would need a piece of dough 8 x 11 inches. Roll the dough (for both tarts and tartlets) to between ⅛-inch and ¹⁄₁₆-inch thick.

To make a circle of dough, roll from the center outward to 12, 6, 3, 9, flap to relax, and then roll to 1:30, 7:30, 4:30 and 9:30.

These directions should be all that is necessary. Make the circle of dough 2 inches in diameter larger than the diameter of the bottom of the tart tin, so a 9½-inch tart tin would need a circle 11½ inches in diameter. Again, roll the dough to between ⅛-inch and ¼-inch thick.

Even some professional bakers have trouble rolling dough into a circle; no matter how they try, they end up with a square. Remember that no one is born knowing how to roll dough into a circle; you learn only through practice, practice, practice...

RELAXING AND AGING PASTRY DOUGH

For a pastry tart shell to be tender and flaky, not tough, the dough must be relaxed and aged. Pastry dough is very much like muscle tissue. As meat from mature cattle must be aged to allow the tension built up from years of exercising to dissipate, so must a pastry dough be relaxed or aged so the tension built up by mixing, kneading and working the dough can dissipate. The first step in this relaxing process is to throw (and I mean *throw*) the dough down on the worktable several times. This also releases air bubbles trapped in the dough, which would cause splits when the dough is rolled (potters use the same procedure to release air bubbles from clay). Wrap the dough securely and refrigerate it for aging. To relax dough after it has been rolled, pick up one end and gently flap it.

REFRIGERATING AND FREEZING
PASTRY DOUGH BEFORE BAKING

Pastry dough can be frozen immediately after it is made (wrap it well) or after it is pressed into the tart tin. If you make a double batch of dough and have two tart tins, by all means press the dough into both tart tins before freezing and save yourself the trouble of rolling the second one out.

If you plan to use the pastry dough within four days after it is made, it will keep under refrigeration. The pressed tart shell, however, always needs to be frozen before baking so it will be rigid and retain its shape while baking. If your freezer is not large enough to accommodate a large tart tin, refrigerate the pressed tart shell until as cold as possible; the baked result, if not excellent, should be good enough.

BRUSHING A TART SHELL WITH EGG WHITE

If a tart must be assembled several hours in advance of serving, to keep it from becoming soggy, brush the fully baked tart shell with an egg white whisked with a little water. Return the tart shell to the oven for 3-5 minutes, or until the egg white has dried.

PRICKING AN UNBAKED TART SHELL

Some pastry doughs should be pricked either before or during baking to release steam. The individual recipes indicate if and when pricking is necessary. Hold a fork perpendicular to the tart shell and prick the bottom in several places.

BAKING PASTRY DOUGH

None of the pastry recipes in this book need those ridiculous beans or aluminum pellets to keep them in shape while baking. I have never used beans or pellets; I have never had to—all my recipes keep their shape with no help. If you have made and formed the dough properly, there is no need for the auxiliary support provided by beans or pellets.

Because of most pastry dough's high fat content, it should be baked very quickly at a high temperature. Always make sure your oven is thoroughly preheated (rely on an oven thermometer). Put the tart tin on a baking sheet, and handle only the baking sheet rather than the tart tin itself (which could result in crumbling the tart shell). Bake until the tart

Common Problems and Solutions to Poor Pastry

Problem	undermixed	overmixed	not enough butter or fat	too much butter or fat	wrong flour	ingredients not cold enough	oven heat too high
Pastry Dough							
too crumbly	●			●	●	●	
tough		●	●		●	●	
difficult to roll		●					
too soft	●		●			●	
Rolled Pastry Tartshell							
crevice							
split rim							
Baked Pastry							
uneven baking							
tough		●	●		●	●	
too light							
too dark							●
excessive shrinkage		●	●		●		
uneven shrinkage		●	●		●		
Double-Baked Tarts							
sticking to pan							
soggy tart shell							

oven heat too low	oven heat uneven	improperly cooled	not aged long enough	not relaxed properly	uneven rolling of dough	overworked dough	hole in the bottom of the tart shell	not enough pounding of the dough	uneven or excessive pinching of rim
			●	●					
			●	●					
								●	
								●	●
	●				●				
●			●	●		●			
●	●								
	●								
			●	●		●			
		●		●	●	●			
		●					●		
●		●					●		

shell is golden brown and seems very dry and set. Many ovens are temperamental and do not heat evenly throughout. If your oven has hot or cool spots, rotate the tart shell while it is baking.

COOLING BAKED PASTRY

Pastry must be thoroughly cooled (all the steam must have evaporated) before you assemble a tart; otherwise, it may not be rigid enough to support the fruit and will become very soggy very quickly. A fast way to cool a tart shell baked in a tart tin with a removable bottom is to set the tart tin on a wide glass or jar and let the ring fall away, exposing the crust edge. Then lift up the tart shell by the metal bottom and place it on a cooling rack. Gently ease away the metal bottom with a palette knife or spatula.

HANDLING BAKED PASTRY

Delicate baked pastry must be handled with extreme gentleness. To transfer a baked tart shell from the tart tin to the serving platter, follow the procedure just described: Set the tart tin on a wide glass or jar and let the metal ring fall away. Then lift up the tart shell by the metal bottom, place it on the serving platter and ease away the metal bottom with a palette knife or spatula. Cutting the tart on the metal bottom can scratch the tin. If a tart baked with a custard filling is stuck to the tart tin, loosen it or ease it out with a palette knife or spatula.

REPAIRING BROKEN TART SHELLS

If a tart shell has split at the edge during baking (it was probably pinched too hard or stretched too much without being relaxed, or the dough was not thrown down on the worktable), make a little sausage of scrap dough and gently press it into the split. Brush the patch with a little beaten egg. Bake about 5 minutes, or until the patch dries and incorporates itself into the other pastry.

To repair a tart shell with a broken rim, use soft butter as glue, piecing together the rim and the rest of the tart shell; brush off the excess butter with a pastry brush. Refrigerate a few minutes until the butter has hardened.

RECYCLING RUINED TART SHELLS

If a tart shell has crumbled beyond repair, it can be recycled into the Crumb Pastry Tart Shell (page 41). Allow the ruined pastry to dry thoroughly by leaving in a warm dry place for several days or in a 250°F oven for about 30 minutes, or until dry. Grind the crumbs in a blender or food processor to a fine and even consistency.

USING A FOOD PROCESSOR
TO MAKE PASTRY DOUGH

A food processor is an excellent tool for making pastry dough; it can mix the dough so quickly that it need never be overworked. Use the steel blade. Make only a single batch of pastry dough at a time because the bowl of the food processor can only hold one batch. If a double batch is needed, do the procedure twice; since it takes only 45 to 60 seconds per batch, the extra time is insignificant.

PASTRY DOUGH SCRAPS

Do not attempt to make another tart shell with leftover scraps of Flaky or Classic Puff Pastry dough; by the time it is rolled again, too much tension will be in the dough and while baking it will relax into a deformed shape. Cut the scraps into strips and sprinkle them with cinnamon and sugar. Bake the little cookies at the temperature specified. The sweet and nut pastries can be rerolled into tartlets, if desired.

MAKING TARTLETS

Tartlets can be made in a myriad of shapes and sizes. For consistency, all the recipes in this book can be used to make six 4-inch-diameter tartlets. Personally, I think one large tart is more dramatic and fun to make than several tartlets. However, some people prefer a whole something on their plates—a whole tartlet to a slice of tart—and tartlets do have the advantage of not requiring slicing. To make tartlets, proceed to roll the dough as directed on page 32. Roll the entire recipe. Cut each tartlet individually with a roll cutter or cleaver (for Classic Puff Pastry Tart Shell, Flaky Pastry Tart Shell and Whole Wheat Flaky Pastry Tart Shell). Ease the dough into the tartlet tins and pinch securely into place (make sure there are no air pockets between the tartlet tin and the dough). Or lay the entire piece of dough on top of the assembled tartlet tins (assembled in a pattern resembling the shape of the dough), roll a rolling pin over the dough to cut it into the appropriate shapes and then pinch the dough into place (for any recipe not mentioned above). Freeze and bake tartlets as you would a large tart. The baking time may be slightly less for tartlets. Check them after 5 minutes of baking time.

CLASSIC PUFF PASTRY TART SHELLS

Feuilletage Classique

Makes one 9-inch round tart or six 4-inch round tartlets

Although time-consuming and a little tricky, this recipe is well worth the effort. Double or triple the quantity and freeze what you do not use.

¼ teaspoon salt
3 tablespoons water
¼ teaspoon lemon juice
½ cup unsalted butter (8 tablespoons or 1 stick)
1 cup sifted and then measured pastry flour (4 ounces)

EGG GLAZE
1 egg
1 tablespoon cream or milk

1. Dissolve the salt in the water and lemon juice. Put in the freezer until very cold but not frozen. It will look like not quite frozen ice cubes.

Hand Method

2. With your hands or a fork, mix 2 tablespoons of the butter with the flour until the mixture forms pealike globules.

3. Pour the cold salt water and lemon juice mixture into the flour all at once and mix until smooth and silky. Continue with Step 4.

Food Processor Method

2. Use the steel blade. Put the flour and 2 tablespoons of the butter in the processor bowl. Process about 10 seconds, until the mixture looks sandy.

3. With the machine running, pour the cold salt water and lemon juice mixture in all at once and process about 30 seconds, until the dough forms a ball.

4. Pat the dough into a 3x5x½-inch rectangle. Wrap securely in plastic wrap and refrigerate 2 hours.

5. Form the remaining butter into a 3x4x½-inch rectangle. Refrigerate about 15 minutes, or until leather-hard (the butter will bend like leather, but will not snap into pieces).

6. On a floured board roll the dough into a 7x8-inch rectangle, following the rolling procedure on page 32. Flap the dough to relax it.

7. Put the butter in the center of the dough and fold the sides of the dough over it to form a sealed envelope. Pound the dough with a rolling pin.

8. Roll out the dough to ¼-inch thick. Flap the dough to relax it. As though you were folding a letter to go into an envelope, fold the right third of the dough down over the center and then fold the left third down. Cover and refrigerate 30 minutes.

9. Repeat the rolling and folding procedure a total of six times. The rolling and folding can be done in sets of two. Be sure to refrigerate 30 minutes between folds. Allow the dough to rest in the refrigerator at least 4 hours or overnight after the six folds have been completed.

10. Roll the dough out to ⅛-inch thick, then refrigerate it for 15 minutes. Mix the egg and cream or milk until smooth.

11. Trim away the edges of the dough with a sharp knife or roll cutter. Do not drag the knife through the dough; this will destroy the layering. Cut the dough into the shape (circle, square, rectangle, diamond or heart) you want for your tart. Cut a concentric piece of dough off ¼ inch from the outer edge; this will be the rim. Brush the outer edge of the dough with egg glaze. Place the rim on the glaze and pinch the two pieces of dough together.

12. Put the shell on a baking sheet lined with parchment or waxed paper (do not butter). Cover securely with plastic wrap and refrigerate for 30 minutes. The tart shell can be frozen at this point; thaw it completely before baking.

13. Preheat the oven to 400°F. Prick the bottom of the tart shell in several places. Brush the tart shell with the egg glaze. Bake about 25–30 minutes, or until golden brown and dry. Cool thoroughly before using.

FLAKY PASTRY TART SHELL

Makes one 9-inch round tart or six 4-inch round tartlets

1½ tablespoons water
¼ teaspoon lemon juice
⅜ cup unsalted butter (6 tablespoons or ¾ stick), cut into ¼-inch cubes -cold
2 teaspoons sugar
¼ teaspoon salt
1 cup sifted and then measured pastry flour (4 ounces)

1. Put the water and the lemon juice in a small bowl in the freezer until very cold but not frozen.

Hand Method

2. Cut the butter into the sugar, salt and flour with a fork or your hands until the mixture forms pealike globules.

3. Pour the water and lemon juice mixture into the flour mixture. Mix until smooth and the dough forms a ball. Continue with Step 4.

Food Processor Method

2. Use the steel blade. Put the butter, sugar, salt and flour in the processor bowl. Process about 15 seconds, until the mixture looks sandy.

3. With the machine running, pour in the water and lemon juice mixture all at once and process about 15 seconds, until the dough forms a ball.

4. Throw the dough down on the worktable several times to release any air pockets. Wrap the dough in plastic and refrigerate for at least 3 (4) hours. or 3-4 d ahead

5. Remove the dough from the refrigerator and allow it to warm to a <u>cool</u> room temperature, or until it is malleable. Press the dough into a flat disk with your hands, and pound it with a rolling pin. to flatten

6. Roll out the dough to ⅛-inch thick on a floured board, following the rolling procedure on page 32. Flap the dough to relax it. more than I care a little

7. Place the dough on the tart tin and ease into the fluted edge. Fold the edges of the dough over to form a double layer on the sides. Pinch the sides together securely and press away any excess dough. Freeze the

For TARTLETS, roll THINNER - don't dbl. Rim

Can use leftover dough pieces but not same day.

5 min may be 95

formed tart shell. Wrap it in plastic if it is to be frozen more than 24 hours.

8. Preheat the oven to 400°F. Put the *frozen* tart tin on a baking sheet and bake about 10 minutes, until the bottom swells. Remove the tart shell from the oven and prick it in several places to release steam. Return it to the oven and bake about another 10 minutes, or until golden brown. Cool thoroughly before using.

7.8 min

WHOLE WHEAT FLAKY PASTRY TART SHELL. Substitute 1 tablespoon brown sugar for the sugar. Increase salt to ½ teaspoon, and use half whole wheat pastry flour and half regular pastry flour.

CRUMB PASTRY TART SHELL

Makes one 9-inch round tart

This pastry is not suitable for tartlets.

1½ cups stale baked goods (graham crackers, cookies, sweet bread, cake, ruined tart shell or combination)
⅜ cup unsalted butter, melted
1 teaspoon grated lemon rind
1 tablespoon sugar (optional; use if the crumbs are not sweet enough for your taste)

1. Let the stale baked goods dry out for a few days in a warm dry place, or in a 250°F oven for 20 minutes.

2. Grind in a food processor or blender until very fine. Sift out and regrind any remaining lumps. Stir together the crumbs, butter, lemon rind and sugar. Refrigerate until it is stiff enough to press into a tart tin.

3. Remove from the refrigerator and press evenly into the tart tin. Freeze. (Wrap in plastic if it is to be frozen more than 24 hours.)

4. Preheat oven to 325°F. Put the tart tin on a baking sheet and bake about 15 minutes, or until set and slightly dry.

5. Cool and release from the tart tin directly to the serving plate.

SWEET PASTRY TART SHELL

Makes one 9-inch round tart or six 4-inch tartlets

Although the Rolling Method takes more words to describe, it is at least four times as fast as the Pressing Method.

⅓ cup unsalted butter
¼ cup sugar
2 egg yolks
1½ cups sifted and then measured all-purpose flour (6 ounces)
Pinch salt

Hand Method

1. Cream the butter and sugar until fluffy, with no lumps remaining.

2. Beat in the egg yolks.

3. Add the flour and salt, a third at a time. Mix until smooth. Pat into a ball. Continue with Step 4.

Food Processor Method

1. Use the steel blade. Put the butter and sugar in the processor bowl. Process about 15 seconds, or until smooth.

2. Stop the machine and add the egg yolks. Process about 10 seconds, or until smooth.

3. Stop the machine and add the flour and salt. Process about 60 seconds, or until the dough forms a ball.

4. Throw the dough on the worktable several times to release any trapped air bubbles. Wrap in plastic and refrigerate 1 hour.

5. Remove the dough from the refrigerator about 5 minutes before rolling or pressing.

Rolling Method

6. Press the dough into a flat disk with your hands. Pound it with a rolling pin. Roll to ⅛-inch thick on a floured board, following the rolling procedure on page 32. Flap the dough to relax it. Place the dough circle on the tart tin. Fold the edges over toward the center to form a double layer at the sides. Pinch the sides together securely and press away any excess dough. Prick the bottom of the tart shell with a fork in several places. Continue with Step 7.

Pressing Method

6. With your fingers, gently press the dough into the tart tin evenly to a ⅛-inch thickness. Prick the bottom of the tart shell with a fork in several places. (Keep pressing until it is even.)

7. Freeze. (Wrap in plastic if the tart shell is to be frozen more than 24 hours.)

8. Preheat the oven to 350°F. Put the tart tin on a baking sheet and bake about 20–25 minutes, or until slightly golden.

9. Allow the tart shell to cool 3 minutes in the tart tin and then release it to a cooling rack.

SWEET CINNAMON PASTRY TART SHELL. Add ½ teaspoon ground cinnamon to the flour.

SWEET LEMON PASTRY TART SHELL. Add ½ teaspoon grated lemon rind to the flour.

NUT PASTRY TART SHELL

Makes one 9-inch tart or six 4-inch round tartlets

An egg yolk makes a softer, shortbread-like tart shell; water or liqueur makes a crunchier tart shell.

¼ cup unsalted butter, cut into ¼-inch cubes
¼ cup sugar
1 cup finely ground almonds or walnuts (4 ounces)
½ cup sifted and then measured all-purpose flour (2 ounces)
½ teaspoon grated lemon rind
1 egg yolk or 1 tablespoon water or liqueur, such as rum
   or Grand Marnier

Hand Method

1. Cream the butter and sugar.

2. Add the nuts, flour and lemon rind. Mix until smooth.

3. Add the egg yolk or liquid. Pat into a ball. Continue with Step 4.

Food Processor Method

1. Use the steel blade. Put the butter and sugar in the processor bowl and process about 15 seconds, until smooth.

2. Stop the machine and add the nuts, flour and lemon rind. Process about 45 seconds, until blended.

3. Stop the machine and add the egg yolk or liquid. Process about 15 seconds, until blended.

4. Wrap the dough in plastic and refrigerate for 1 hour.

5. Remove from the refrigerator and press the dough evenly into the tart tin. Refrigerate about 15 minutes, or until stiff.

6. Preheat the oven to 350°F.

7. Put the tart tin on a baking sheet and bake about 20–25 minutes, until golden brown.

8. Cool 3 minutes in the tart tin, and then release the tart shell to a cooling rack.

CINNAMON NUT PASTRY TART SHELL. Add ½ teaspoon ground cinnamon to the flour.

CHOCOLATE NUT PASTRY TART SHELL. Substitute 2 tablespoons cocoa for 2 tablespoons flour.

MERINGUE TART SHELL

Makes one 9-inch tart or six 4-inch round tartlets

This tart shell does not require a tart tin. It is lighter than a pastry tart shell and can be used with any pastry cream (except hollandaise) and fruit.

¼ cup egg whites (from about 2 large eggs)
¼ cup granulated sugar (2 ounces)
¼ cup sifted and then measured powdered sugar (1 ounce)

1. Preheat oven to 300°F.

2. Draw a circle 9 inches in diameter (for tartlets, six circles 4 inches in diameter) on a piece of waxed paper or parchment. Lay the paper, pencil side down, on a baking sheet. Butter and sugar (use granulated sugar here) the paper.

3. Beat the egg whites with the sugar until very stiff (the peaks should not fall over). Fold in the powdered sugar. Blend only until smooth. *Do not overmix.*

4. Put the mixture in a large pastry bag fitted with a ½-inch plain nozzle tip.

5. Pipe a disk ¼-inch thick inside the circle (or circles) drawn on the paper. Smooth the disk with a palette knife. Pipe a rim along the outside edge, topped by another layer of meringue to make a wall.

6. Bake until dry, about 1½ hours, or turn the oven off after 30 minutes and leave the tart shell in the oven overnight (do not open the oven door to peek).

7. Use immediately or store in a dry, airtight container for up to several weeks.

Note. Exercise extreme gentleness when handling; meringue is very brittle. Assemble the tart only at the last minute; meringue gets soggy very quickly.

NUT MERINGUE TART SHELL. Add ⅓ cup finely ground nuts to the powdered sugar before folding it into the egg whites.

COCOA MERINGUE TART SHELL. Sift 1 tablespoon packed cocoa into the powdered sugar before folding it into the egg whites.

CHOCOLATE PASTRY TART SHELL

Makes one 9-inch or six 4-inch tartlets

1¼ cups sifted and then measured all-purpose flour (5 ounces)
2 tablespoons packed cocoa
⅓ cup unsalted butter
⅓ cup sugar
2 egg yolks

Sift the flour and cocoa together and follow the procedure for Sweet Pastry Tart Shell (page 42).

COCONUT PASTRY TART SHELL

Makes one 9-inch tart or six 4-inch round tartlets

¼ cup unsalted butter
¼ cup sugar
1 cup grated, dried, unsweetened coconut (3 ounces)
½ cup sifted and then measured all-purpose flour (2 ounces)
½ teaspoon grated lemon rind
1 egg yolk or 1 tablespoon water or liqueur, such as rum
   or Grand Marnier.

Hand Method

1. Cream the butter and sugar.

2. Add the coconut, flour and lemon rind. Mix until smooth.

3. Add the egg yolk or liquid. Pat into a ball. Continue with Step 4.

Food Processor Method

1. Use the steel blade. Put the butter and sugar in the processor bowl and process about 15 seconds, or until smooth.

2. Stop the machine and add the coconut, flour and lemon rind. Process about 45 seconds, or until blended.

3. Stop the machine and add the egg yolk or liquid. Process about 15 seconds, or until blended.

4. Wrap the dough in plastic and refrigerate for 1 hour.

5. Remove from the refrigerator and press the dough evenly into the tart tin. Refrigerate about 15 minutes, or until stiff.

6. Preheat the oven to 350°F. Put the tart tin on a baking sheet and bake about 20–25 minutes, or until slightly golden.

7. Cool 3 minutes in the tart tin, and then release the tart shell to a cooling rack.

Note. As in the Nut Pastry Tart Shell (page 44), an egg yolk makes a softer, shortbread-like tart shell; water or liqueur makes a crunchier tart shell.

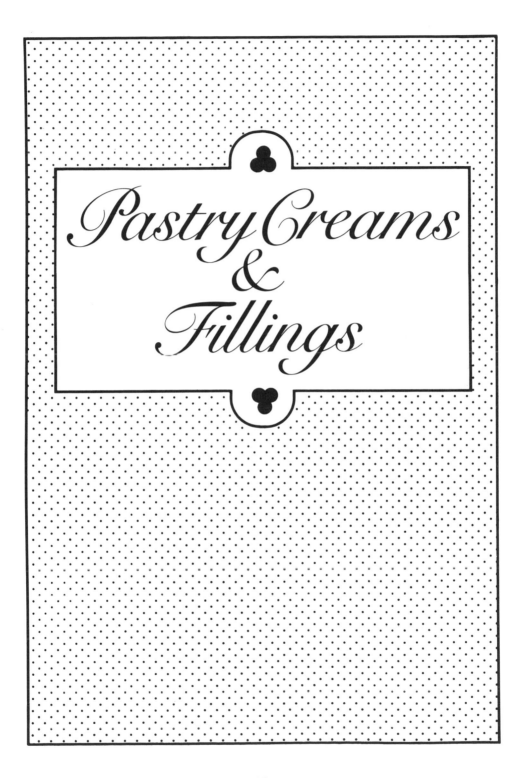

Pastry Creams
&
Fillings

P astry cream is an intermediary between the crust and the fruit; it adds smoothness and complements the flavors of each.

The recipes for cooked pastry cream make enough for two or three tarts, because it is impossible to make a very small amount without scorching it.

There is only one secret to a great pastry cream: fresh cream!

TEMPERATURE OF INGREDIENTS

To shorten the cooking time of custard-based pastry creams, have the ingredients at room temperature.

LUMPY PASTRY CREAM

To avoid lumpy pastry cream, make sure the sugar and eggs are mixed together well. Also, the water in the bottom of the double boiler shouldn't be too hot or the egg yolks will become scrambled. If you end up with lumpy pastry cream, homogenize it for a few seconds in a blender or food processor with a metal knife. If all else fails, give it to your favorite cat.

PREVENTING A SKIN FROM FORMING ON A PASTRY CREAM

Sometimes, a skin forms on top of the pastry cream which ruins the smooth texture of the pastry cream. To prevent this, stir the pastry cream occasionally until it has cooled, press a piece of plastic wrap directly on the surface of the pastry cream (not just on top of the container) or pour a little cream on the pastry cream; it can be stirred into the rest when set.

. . . .

NO-COOK PASTRY CREAMS

The no-cook pastry creams, although not as full-bodied and rich-tasting as the other recipes, are very good for those occasions when you are in a hurry. They will keep as long as sour cream, yogurt and cream cheese normally would, about a week (always smell week-old pastry creams and discard if it smells rancid). The no-cook pastry creams may be varied just like the other recipes.

STORING PASTRY CREAM

Because of the high fat and sugar content of most pastry creams, they can sour relatively quickly. Store all pastry creams well sealed in the refrigerator. Always smell a pastry cream if it has been in storage more than a few days to make sure it has not soured.

. . . .

CLASSIC PASTRY CREAM

Makes 1½ cups (enough for 2-3 tarts)

It is impossible to properly cook an amount less than this. Refrigerate any leftovers for another tart.

1 cup heavy cream
3 tablespoons sugar (preferably vanilla sugar, page 18)
2 egg yolks
1 tablespoon cornstarch
1-inch piece vanilla bean or ¼ teaspoon vanilla extract

1. Warm ¾ cup of the cream in the top of a double boiler over simmering but not boiling water.

2. Stir the sugar into the egg yolks and add the cornstarch.

3. Split the vanilla bean with a knife. Scrape out the sticky, brown, inner specks and add them to the yolk mixture, or add the vanilla extract.

4. Add the yolk mixture to the warm cream. Cook, mixing constantly with a wire whisk, until the mixture thickens and the whisk marks keep their shape (160°F). Scrape the sides of the pot if the mixture is sticking.

....

5. Remove from the heat and add the remaining ¼ cup cream. Whisk ^(to stop the cooking) occasionally until cool (this prevents a skin from forming on the top of the pastry cream).

6. Cover with plastic wrap and store in the refrigerator for up to a week.

Note. Do not discard the vanilla bean. Use it to make more vanilla sugar (page 18).

....

PASTRY CREAM MADE WITH MILK

Makes 1½ cups (enough for 2–3 tarts)

1 cup whole milk
3 tablespoons unsalted butter
¼ cup sugar
1½ tablespoons sifted and then measured cornstarch
¼ cup egg yolks (about 3)
1-inch piece vanilla bean or ¼ teaspoon vanilla extract

1. Put the milk and butter in the top of a double boiler over simmering but not boiling water.

2. Mix the sugar and cornstarch and then blend in the egg yolks. Split the vanilla bean and scrape out the sticky, dark brown, tiny inner specks into the yolk mixture, or add the vanilla extract. Pour into the warm milk and cook, mixing constantly with a wire whisk, until thick and the whisk marks keep their shape (160°F). Remove from the heat and whisk occasionally until cool (this prevents a skin from forming on top).

3. Cover and store in the refrigerator for up to a week.

ALCOHOLIC PASTRY CREAM. Substitute 2 tablespoons liqueur (kirschwasser, Grand Marnier, brandy or cognac) for 2 tablespoons of the heavy cream, adding only after the pastry cream has cooled.

PRALINE PASTRY CREAM. Add ¼ cup praline (page 60) to the pastry cream before refrigerating.

53

ANGELICA PASTRY CREAM. Add 1 tablespoon chopped candied angelica root to the pastry cream before refrigerating.

ANISETTE PASTRY CREAM. Add a dash of Pernod to the pastry cream before refrigerating.

TAMARIND PASTRY CREAM. Add 1 teaspoon tamarind pulp to the pastry cream before refrigerating.

NUT PASTRY CREAM. Fold in ½ cup (2 ounces) of finely ground toasted nuts (almonds, walnuts, pistachio nuts, hazelnuts or pecans) before spreading the cream on the tart.

CHOCOLATE PASTRY CREAM. Add ⅓ cup (1 ounce) grated bittersweet chocolate when the cream is being thickened in the double boiler.

SPICE PASTRY CREAM. Fold in ¼ teaspoon each freshly ground cinnamon and freshly grated nutmeg before putting the cream in the refrigerator to set.

PASTRY CREAM MADE WITH SOUR CREAM

Makes ½ cup (enough for 1 tart)

½ cup sour cream (4 ounces)
2-3 tablespoons vanilla sugar (page 18)
1-2 tablespoons Grand Marnier

Blend until smooth.

PASTRY CREAM MADE WITH YOGURT

Makes ½ cup (enough for 1 tart)

½ cup whole-milk yogurt (4 ounces)
2–3 tablespoons vanilla sugar (page 18)
1–2 teaspoons Grand Marnier

Blend until smooth.

PASTRY CREAM MADE WITH CREAM CHEESE

Makes ½ cup (enough for 1 tart)

⅓ cup cream cheese (3 ounces), at room temperature
2 tablespoons honey or praline (page 60)
1–2 tablespoons Grand Marnier

Blend until smooth.

....

HOLLANDAISE PASTRY FILLING

Makes 1 cup or enough for one 9-inch tart

Do not be alarmed—this is not the same hollandaise that you serve with asparagus; it is pastry hollandaise, a classical filling featuring blanched almonds.

⅜ cup unsalted butter (3 ounces)
⅜ cup sugar (3 ounces)
¾ cup packed finely ground blanched almonds (3 ounces)
1 large egg (¼ cup scant)
¼ cup sifted and then measured all-purpose flour (1 ounce)
1 tablespoon grated lemon rind

Hand Method

1. Cream the butter and sugar until fluffy and no lumps remain.

2. Beat in the almonds and then the egg, flour and lemon rind. Beat until no lumps remain.

Food Processor Method

1. Use the steel blade. Put the butter and sugar in the processor bowl. Process about 15 seconds, or until smooth.

2. Add the egg and process about 15 seconds, until smooth. Add the almonds, flour and lemon rind and process about 20 seconds, or until smooth.

Note. This filling can be stored up to two weeks if well covered in the refrigerator. Allow it to come to a soft consistency before spreading onto the tart shell.

LEMON CUSTARD

Makes enough for 1 tart

⅓ cup sugar
2 tablespoons sifted and then measured cornstarch
3 tablespoons cream
⅓ cup egg yolks (from about 4 large eggs)
4 tablespoons grated lemon rind
⅓ cup lemon juice
⅓ cup unsalted butter
1 large egg

1. Sift together the sugar and cornstarch. Beat in the cream and the egg yolks, then add the lemon rind and juice. Blend until smooth. Add the butter.

2. Whisking constantly, cook the mixture in the top of a double boiler over simmering but not boiling water for about 10 minutes, until slightly thick or at 140°F.

3. Remove from the heat and beat in the egg. Cool (continue whisking while cooling).

4. Cover securely if the custard is to be stored. This custard may be prepared several days in advance and will keep at least a week well sealed in the refrigerator.

LIME CUSTARD. Substitute lime rind and juice for the lemon rind and juice.

ORANGE CUSTARD. Substitute orange rind and juice for the lemon rind and juice.

....

CUSTARD FOR COOKED TARTS

Use this recipe in apple, apricot, Italian plum and rhubarb tarts.

Makes enough for 1 tart.

¼ cup heavy cream (2 ounces)
¼ cup Classic Pastry Cream (page 52) (other pastry creams are not
  suitable)
1 large egg (about ¼ cup)
2 tablespoons finely ground nuts (¼ ounce)

Blend until smooth.

....

FRANGIPANE

Makes enough for 1 tart

This is a classical pastry filling featuring blanched almonds.

½ cup packed very finely ground blanched almonds (4 ounces)
1 cup sifted and then measured confectioner's sugar (4 ounces)
1 egg white
1 whole egg
2 tablespoons unsalted butter (1 ounce), melted
1 teaspoon grated lemon rind

1. Blend the almonds, sugar, egg white and whole egg to form a paste.

2. Beat in the butter and lemon rind until smooth.

3. This filling will keep up to a week in a covered jar in the refrigerator.

CRUSHED ALMOND MACAROON FILLING

Makes 2 dozen 1-inch round macaroons

Crushed macaroons add a pleasant depth of flavor and crunchiness to fruit tarts. Use Amaretti Lazzaroni, the Italian almond macaroons that come in bright red cans and are available in import stores, or make your own.

¼ cup egg whites (from 2–3 large eggs)
¾ cup sugar (6 ounces)
1½ cups finely ground unblanched almonds (6 ounces)
1 tablespoon grated lemon rind

1. Preheat oven to 325°F.

2. Line two 12×18-inch baking sheets with waxed or parchment paper. Butter the paper and sprinkle sugar over it.

3. Beat the egg whites with the sugar until the peaks keep their shape but fall over slightly into a graceful hook.

4. Fold in the almonds and the lemon rind, a third at a time. Blend only until smooth. *Do not overmix.*

5. Drop spoonfuls of the batter onto the prepared baking sheets, or pipe through a pastry bag fitted with a ½-inch nozzle tip, 1 inch apart.

6. Bake about 20 minutes, or until set.

7. Loosen from the paper with a palette knife. Stored unrefrigerated in an airtight container, these macaroons will keep several weeks.

8. To crush macaroons, put them between two pieces of waxed or parchment paper and crush with a rolling pin until they become powdery, or simply crush them with the underside of a spoon or in a food processor.

9. Use about ¼ cup crushed macaroons for each 9-inch tart.

PRALINE

Makes ½ cup

½ cup sugar (4 ounces)
¼ cup unblanched whole or slivered almonds (1 ounce)

1. Oil a piece of marble at least 9 x 9 inches, or a 9-inch round cake pan. (Use a bland vegetable oil, such as safflower or corn; butter does not work well.)

2. Put the sugar in a heavy saucepan or skillet. Melt the sugar until it turns golden brown. Add the almonds.

3. Quickly pour this mixture onto the marble or the cake pan and allow it to harden. Be extremely careful when handling the hot sugar.

4. When it has cooled, put the praline on paper towel to absorb any excess oil.

5. To use, grind the praline to a powder in a blender or food processor. To store praline, do not grind it; simply break it up into pieces and put in an airtight, *absolutely moisture-free* container. Praline will keep for several months at a cool room temperature.

Glazes

....

A glaze dresses up the appearance of a tart, preserves the flavor and adds a depth of flavor of its own. The glaze flavor specified in each recipe is just a suggestion. Feel free to invent new combinations. Just be sure that the flavors of the fruit and the glaze do not clash and the glaze color does not dominate the fruit color. For maximum taste, make your own glazes from fresh fruit; they are very easy to make. Glazes must be stored in the refrigerator, frozen or sealed in sterilized jars, like jelly. Some of the recipes leave some jam to spread on toast. Use 3 tablespoons to ¼ cup glaze for each fruit tart.

STERILIZING JARS TO STORE GLAZE

Use only jars that can be vacuum-sealed—those with metal clamps or lids and rings, free of defects such as chips or cracks that could prevent a seal. Wash the jars with soap and water. Put the jars in a large pot and cover with water. Boil for 10 minutes. Meanwhile, heat the glaze if it has cooled. Remove the jars from the water with tongs and immediately pour the hot glaze through a funnel, leaving ½ inch headspace. Carefully lift the funnel so no glaze spills onto the rim of the jar. Dip the round metal lid in the hot water and place it on top of the jar. Immediately tighten the metal ring onto the jar, or clamp down the metal clamp. The lid will seem swollen for about 30 minutes and will then "pop." This pop signifies that the air trapped inside has been released and a perfect vacuum seal has been formed. Store the glaze in a cool place away from light, which causes the color of the glaze to fade.

USING STORE-BOUGHT JAM, JELLY AND PRESERVES AS GLAZE

To use store-bought jam, jelly or preserves for glaze, heat it in a heavy saucepan and strain through a jelly bag or wire mesh strainer. Allow it to cool slightly before brushing onto the tart.

HONEY GLAZE

Honey can also be used as a glaze. Use only mildly flavored honey that will not mask or interfere with the flavors of the fruit. Heat the honey slightly to a brushable consistency.

ADDING ALCOHOL TO A GLAZE

Lacing glaze with alcohol—brandy, rum or Grand Marnier—can add flavor. Add one teaspoon alcohol to ¼ cup glaze after the glaze is cooled.

HEATING GLAZE

A glaze may be too stiff to be readily brushable. Heat it in a heavy saucepan or in a double boiler until it is liquid enough.

SPRITZING A TART WITH ALCOHOL

A little liqueur or brandy brings out the flavor in any fruit. Choose a liqueur brandy that complements the fruit you are using, such as Grand Marnier with citrus fruit, kirschwasser with cherries or Calvados with apples. The amount specified in each recipe is conservative; spritz on more if you like. Do not do this until immediately before the tart is served, or it will get soggy very quickly.

APPLE GLAZE

Makes 1–2 cups

1 pound tart apples (about 2 large), such as Pippin, Gravenstein or
   Granny Smith
2 cups water
1–2 cups sugar
1 teaspoon lemon juice

1. Rinse apples and remove the pip end and stem. (Do not core or remove
the seeds.) Chop into ¼-inch cubes.

2. Put the chopped apples and water in a heavy saucepan. Boil about 30
minutes, until the apples become a mushy pulp.

3. Strain the apple pulp, without squeezing, through a jelly bag.

4. Measure the juice. Put it in a heavy saucepan and add an equal
amount of sugar and the lemon juice.

5. Bring to a full boil while stirring, being careful that the mixture does
not boil over. Turn the heat down to a simmer and cook about 20–25
minutes, or until a spoonful of the glaze becomes set or jellylike after 5
minutes in the refrigerator. Skim off the foam.

6. Seal in sterilized jars (see page 63) or store in the refrigerator or
freezer.

APRICOT GLAZE

Makes ¾ cup glaze and ¾ cup thick jam

1½ cups apricots, washed, pitted and cut into ½-inch cubes
1½ cups sugar

1. Put the apricots and sugar in a heavy saucepan. Mash with a fork until all the sugar is dissolved. Bring to a full boil while stirring, being careful that the mixture does not boil over. Turn the heat down to a simmer and cook about 20–25 minutes, or until a spoonful of the mixture becomes set or jellylike after 5 minutes in the refrigerator. Skim off the foam.

2. Strain, without squeezing, through a jelly bag or strainer. The part that drips through is the glaze; the rest is jam.

3. Seal in sterilized jars (see page 63) or store in the refrigerator or freezer.

CHOCOLATE GLAZE

Makes enough for 1 tart

8 ounces bittersweet chocolate (see Note)
¼ cup heavy cream
3 tablespoons unsalted butter

1. Chop very finely or grate the chocolate. Put the chocolate and cream in the top of a double boiler over hot but *not boiling* water. Stir with a chopstick until melted. Stir in the butter.

2. Put the tart to be glazed on a cooling rack set on a baking sheet to catch the excess glaze. When the glaze has cooled to 96°F, or until a drop of the glaze will not spread on a plate, pour it on the tart. (Strain it first if it seems lumpy.) Pick up the baking sheet and drop it from a height of 3 inches to level the glaze. Let the tart sit on the rack 30 minutes while the glaze sets. Transfer the tart to a serving plate.

Note. Chocolate is not chocolate is not chocolate! Do not use inferior chocolate for this recipe. Although simple and easy, this recipe will not be as good with just any type of chocolate. Recommended brands are Lindt Excellence (Swiss), Tobler Tradition (Swiss), Godiva Sweet Cooking Chocolate (U.S.A.), Ghiradelli Bittersweet (U.S.A.), Guittard Bittersweet (U.S.A.). See the Mail Order Guide (page 133) if these brands are unavailable in your area.

CITRUS GLAZE

Makes 1⅓ cups

1 cup freshly squeezed citrus juice
1 cup sugar

1. Put the juice and sugar in a heavy saucepan. Bring to a full boil while stirring, being careful that the mixture does not boil over. Turn the heat down to a low boil and cook about 30 minutes, or until a spoonful of the glaze becomes set or jellylike after 5 minutes in the refrigerator. Skim off the foam.

2. Seal in sterilized jars (see page 63) or store in the refrigerator or freezer.

PEACH GLAZE

Makes 1 cup

2 large or 3 small peaches, peeled, pitted and cut into ¼-inch cubes
1 cup sugar
1 tablespoon lemon juice

1. Mash the peaches with a fork, or grind in a blender or food processor. Measure 1 cup of the peach pulp.

2. Put the pulp, sugar and lemon juice in a heavy saucepan. Bring to a full boil while stirring, being careful that the mixture does not boil over. Turn the heat down to a low boil and cook about 20–25 minutes, or until a spoonful of the mixture becomes set or jellylike after 5 minutes in the refrigerator. Skim off the foam.

3. Seal in sterilized jars (see page 63) or store in the refrigerator or freezer.

PLUM GLAZE

Makes ¾ cup glaze and ¾ cup thick jam

1½ cups prune type or Italian plums, rinsed and cut into ½-inch cubes
1½ cups sugar

1. Put the plums and sugar in a heavy saucepan. Mash with a fork until all the sugar is dissolved. Bring to a full boil while stirring, being careful that the mixture does not boil over. Turn the heat down to a low boil and cook about 20–25 minutes, or until a spoonful of the mixture becomes set or jellylike after 5 minutes in the refrigerator. Skim off the foam.

2. Strain, without squeezing, through a jelly bag or strainer. The part that drips through is the glaze; the rest is jam.

3. Seal in sterilized jars (see page 63) or store in the refrigerator or freezer.

RASPBERRY GLAZE

Makes 1 cup glaze and ½ cup thick jam

2 cups raspberries (about 1 pint)
2 cups sugar
1 tablespoon lemon juice

1. If the raspberries are dirty or dusty, rinse them off; otherwise do not.

2. Put the raspberries, sugar and lemon juice in a heavy saucepan. Mash with a fork until all the sugar is dissolved. Bring to a full boil while stirring, being careful that the mixture does not boil over. Turn the heat down to a low boil and cook about 20 minutes, or until a spoonful of the mixture becomes set or jellylike after 5 minutes in the refrigerator. Skim off the foam.

3. Strain, without squeezing, through a jelly bag or strainer. The part that drips through is the glaze; the rest is jam.

4. Seal in sterilized jars (see page 63) or store in the refrigerator or freezer.

STRAWBERRY GLAZE

Makes 1 cup

1 pint slightly underripe strawberries
1 cup sugar
1 teaspoon lemon juice

1. Wash and stem the strawberries. Squeeze them through a jelly bag (save the pulp for spreading on toast). Measure 1 cup of the juice.

2. Put the strawberry juice, sugar and lemon juice in a heavy saucepan. Bring to a full boil while stirring, being careful that the mixture does not boil over. Turn the heat down to a low boil and cook about 30 minutes, or until a spoonful of the glaze becomes set or jellylike after 5 minutes in the refrigerator. Skim off the foam.

3. Seal in sterilized jars (see page 63) or store in the refrigerator or freezer.

Fruit Tarts

A ll the following tarts can be cut into six large or eight good-sized servings; the same amount of pastry cream and fruit will make six 4-inch round tartlets.

Each recipe specifies how long before serving the particular tart may be assembled; otherwise, the pastry cream may saturate the crust, resulting in a soggy mess.

If your room temperature is higher than about 65°F, refrigerate the tart, but allow it to return to room temperature before serving.

The following recipes do not constitute a finite list of all possible fruit tart creations. If there is a particular fruit indigenous to your area, by all means, make a tart with it!

ARRANGING A FRUIT TART

Making a beautiful fruit tart can be a very rewarding and sensual experience. The design possibilities are almost endless, and if one particular design fails, the tart will soon be eaten and another can be made another day. The designs given in the recipes are just suggestions that allow you to calculate the amount of fruit needed. Specific methods for arranging the fruit as pictured in the diagrams are contained within each recipe. If a fruit can be sliced into more than one kind of segment, experiment with a new shape, or combine it with an old shape. Keep in mind how the tart will be sliced.

Always start arranging the fruit at the outside edge and work toward the center; it does not matter if the design center does not fall in the geometric center of the tart, but it does matter if the last concentric ring of fruit is not parallel to the outside edge. Overlap the fruit segments to cover all the pastry cream or the bottom of the tart shell. A sloppy bit of pastry cream leaking through the fruit can ruin the dramatic effect of the glorious fruit neatly arranged. Choose a color of glaze that complements the fruit, that does not overpower it and mask the color. If the strawberries you used were pale and not as flavorful as you hoped, you can even cheat a little bit by brushing the tart with a deeply colored and strongly flavored raspberry glaze.

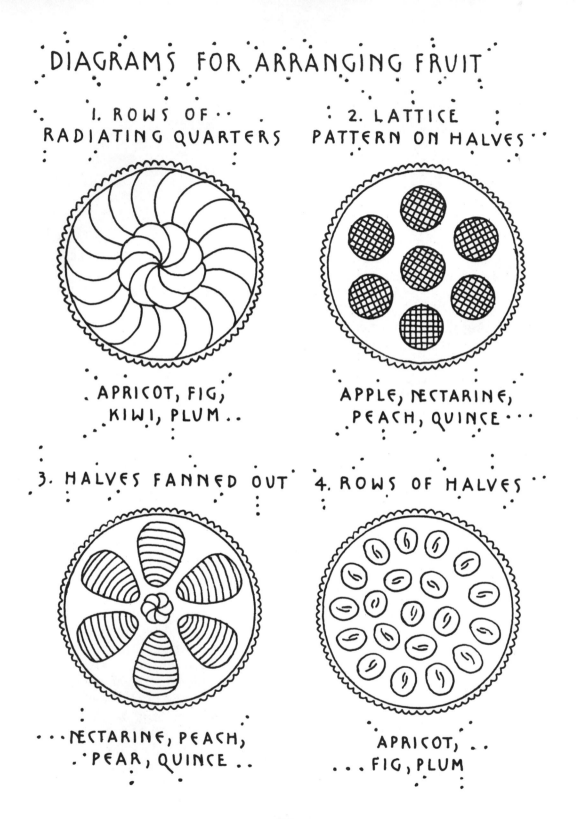

DIAGRAMS FOR ARRANGING FRUIT

1. ROWS OF RADIATING QUARTERS

APRICOT, FIG, KIWI, PLUM

2. LATTICE PATTERN ON HALVES

APPLE, NECTARINE, PEACH, QUINCE

3. HALVES FANNED OUT

NECTARINE, PEACH, PEAR, QUINCE

4. ROWS OF HALVES

APRICOT, FIG, PLUM

5. LATTICE CENTER WITH RADIATING SLICES

APPLE, NECTARINE, PEACH, PEAR, QUINCE

6. OVERLAPPING ROUND SLICES

BANANA, KIWI, PERSIMMON

7. CAMELLIA PATTERN

APPLE, APRICOT, GRAPEFRUIT, NECTARINE, ORANGE, PAPAYA, PEACH, PEAR, PINEAPPLE, QUINCE

The lights are low; the flickering of a candle flame or a nearby fire is reflected on the glaze of the fruit. The minds and palates of one and all are satisfied after an evening of good conversation and food and drink. The senses are stimulated yet relaxed. One feels but a vague longing for a finishing touch—it is too beautiful to be cut! To destroy its geometric unity would be blasphemous. The nose and salivary glands get the better of the mind's pleasure in abstract geometric unity; it is cut (cleanly, with a sharp knife). A flat wedge-shaped serving tool is eased underneath each slice, transferring it to the serving plates (of any fine material except aluminum or scratched silver plate). The lights are still low; the music sweet; the coffee strong and black; the Sauterne sweet or the champagne dry. The flavors of the fruit tart erupt, so neatly married (the flaky, buttery crust, the smooth, viscous pastry cream, the fruit captured in its moment of excellence and glory); simple but of great and most delicate beauty.

APPLE TART WITH CLASSIC PUFF PASTRY

Baked Classic Puff Pastry Tart Shell (page 38)
1 pound tart apples, such as Pippin, Gravenstein or Granny Smith (about 2 large or 3 small)
½ cup Apricot Glaze (page 66)

1. Preheat the oven to 350°F.

2. Put the tart shell on a baking sheet lined with waxed or parchment paper.

3. Peel, halve and core the apples. Lay the apple halves flat and slice into ⅛-inch segments across the width.

4. Arrange the slices on the tart shell, starting at the outside edge and working toward the center, overlapping slightly in a camellia pattern (diagram 7, page 75). Brush the apples with a little glaze.

5. Bake 15 minutes. Remove from the oven and brush with a little more glaze. Return to the oven and bake about another 15 minutes, until the edges of the apples get brown. Remove from the baking sheet to a cooling rack.

6. Brush with a little more glaze.

7. Serve within 3 hours.

APPLE TART WITH FLAKY PASTRY

Baked Flaky Pastry Tart Shell (page 40)
1 pound tart apples, such as Pippin, Gravenstein or Granny Smith
(about 2 large or 3 small)
Custard for Cooked Tarts (page 58)
½ cup Apricot Glaze (page 66)

1. Preheat the oven to 350°F.

2. Leave the tart shell in the tart tin and put it on a baking sheet.

3. Peel, halve and core the apples.

Method 1

4. Lay the apple halves flat and slice into ⅛-inch segments across the width. Arrange the slices in the tart shell, starting at the opposite edge and working toward the center, overlapping slightly in a camellia pattern (diagram 7, page 75). Continue with step 5.

Method 2

4. Reserve one apple half and score a lattice pattern halfway through it. Lay the remaining apple halves flat and slice them into ⅛-inch segments across the width. Put the half in the center of the tart shell and arrange the slices so they radiate from it, overlapping slightly (diagram 5, page 75). Continue with step 5.

Method 3

4. Score a lattice pattern halfway through the apple halves. Arrange the apple halves in the tart shell (diagram 2, page 74).

5. Pour the custard on top of the apples and let it drip through. Brush a little glaze on the apples.

6. Bake for 15 minutes. Remove from the oven and brush more glaze on the apples. Return to the oven and bake about another 15 minutes, or until the edges of the apples get brown. Remove from the oven and immediately release from the tart tin to a cooling rack.

7. Brush with a little more glaze.

8. Serve within 5 hours.

VARIATIONS
Instead of the Flaky Pastry Tart Shell try:
Whole Wheat Flaky Pastry Tart Shell (page 41)

APPLE AND JAM TART

10 ounces apples (1 large or 2 small)
1 cup jam or marmalade (strawberry, raspberry, apricot or orange)
2 tablespoons grated lemon rind (optional)
Unbaked Nut Pastry Tart Shell (page 44)

1. Preheat the oven to 350°F.

2. Peel, halve, core and grate the apples. Measure 1 cup.

3. Mix the apples with the jam or marmalade and lemon rind. Pour into the tart shell.

4. Put the tart tin on a baking sheet and bake about 25-30 minutes, until the tart shell has browned slightly and the jam seems set.

5. Immediately release the tart to a cooling rack.

6. Serve within 10 hours.

....

APPLE TART WITH HOLLANDAISE

Baked Flaky Pastry Tart Shell (page 40)
¾ pound tart apples, such as Pippin, Gravenstein or Granny Smith
  (2 large or 3 small)
¼ cup Apricot Glaze (page 66)
Hollandaise Pastry Filling (page 56), at room temperature
1-2 tablespoons brandy (optional)
Powdered sugar
Paper doily or stencil pattern

1. Preheat the oven to 350°F.

2. Leave the tart shell in the tart tin and put it on a baking sheet.

3. Peel, halve and core the apples. Lay the apple halves flat and slice them into ⅛-inch segments.

4. Brush the bottom of the tart shell with a little glaze. Spread half the hollandaise on the tart shell. Press the apple segments into the hollandaise and spread the remaining hollandaise on the apples.

5. Bake about 35-40 minutes, or until golden brown. Release the tart to a cooling rack. When cooled, spritz on the brandy.

6. Place the doily or stencil pattern on top of the tart. Sprinkle the powdered sugar through the doily as a decorative garnish.

7. Serve within 8 hours.

TARTE TATIN

A very easy, "upside down" apple tart.

Unbaked Flaky Pastry Tart Shell dough rolled into a 10½-inch round piece
¼ cup unsalted butter
¾ cup sugar
1½ pounds tart apples (3 large or 5 small)
2–3 tablespoons Calvados or Brandy (optional)

1. Preheat the oven to 350°F.

2. Melt the butter and pour it into a 9-inch round (pyrex is preferable) cake pan. (Do not use a tart tin or spring-form pan; the sugar will leak out and burn on the bottom of your oven, a formidable mess!)

3. Peel, halve and core the apples and slice them into ⅛-inch segments along the length.

4. In a heavy saucepan over medium heat, melt the sugar until golden brown. Pour it over the butter in the cake pan and pile on the apple segments. Sprinkle on the liqueur if desired.

5. Put the dough over the apples tucking the edges down around the sides of the pan. Prick the dough with a fork in 5 or 6 places.

6. Bake until the tart shell pastry is golden brown, about 35–40 minutes. Immediately invert the tart onto a serving plate. Spritz on more liqueur if desired and serve while still warm.

APRICOT TART

Baked Flaky Pastry Tart Shell (page 40)
¾ pound apricots (about 6 medium)
Custard for Cooked Tarts (page 58)
¾ cup Apricot Glaze (page 66)
¼ cup chopped pistachio nuts (optional)
1-2 teaspoons kirschwasser or brandy (optional)

1. Preheat the oven to 350°F.

2. Leave the tart shell in the tart tin and put it on a baking sheet.

3. Wash the apricots, halve along the length, and pit.

Method 1

4. Arrange the apricot halves, skin side down, in a row radiating toward the center. Arrange the next row in a ring, and fill the center with another radiating row (diagram 4, page 74). Continue with Step 5.

Method 2

4. Quarter the apricots by slicing the halves along the length. Arrange the quarters starting in a row radiating toward the center, overlapping slightly. Arrange the next row radiating in the opposite direction (diagram 1, page 74). Continue with Step 5.

Method 3

4. Quarter the apricots by slicing the halves along the length. Arrange the quarters by starting at the outside edge and working toward the center, overlapping slightly in a camellia pattern (diagram 7, page 75).

5. Pour the custard around the apricots. Brush with a little glaze.

6. Bake for 15 minutes. Remove the tart from the oven and brush with a little glaze. Return to the oven and bake about another 15 minutes, or until the edges of the apricots get brown. Remove from the oven and immediately release from the tart tin to a cooling rack.

7. Brush the entire surface of the tart (not just the apricots) with glaze.

Sprinkle the nuts into the wells of the apricots if you followed Method 1; otherwise just randomly. Spritz with the kirschwasser or brandy.

8. Serve within 3 hours.

BLUEBERRY TART

1 pound blueberries (about 1 pint)
¼ cup Raspberry Glaze (page 69)
Baked Flaky Pastry Tart Shell (page 40)
½ cup Classic Pastry Cream (page 52) or any plain pastry cream
1-2 teaspoons kirschwasser (optional)

1. Rinse the blueberries. Put them in a heavy saucepan with the glaze. Poach about 5 minutes, or until some of the berries begin to pop. Drain and cool thoroughly.

2. Put the tart shell on the serving plate. Spread the pastry cream over the tart shell.

3. Spoon the berries over the pastry cream.

4. Spritz with kirschwasser.

5. Serve within 2 hours.

VARIATIONS
Instead of the Flaky Pastry Tart Shell try:
Whole Wheat Flaky Pastry Tart Shell (page 41)
Classic Puff Pastry Tart Shell (page 38)
Nut Pastry Tart Shell (page 44)
Meringue (page 45), Nut Meringue (page 46) or Cocoa Meringue (page 46) Tart Shell (assemble only at the last minute)

Instead of Classic Pastry Cream try:
Praline Pastry Cream (page 53)
Nut Pastry Cream (page 54)
Alcoholic Pastry Cream (page 53) with brandy
Or omit pastry cream and sprinkle ¼ cup Crushed Almond Macaroon Filling (page 59) on the tart shell before spooning on the blueberries.

BANANA TART

Baked Flaky Pastry Tart Shell (page 40)
½ cup Classic Pastry Cream (page 52) or any plain pastry cream
1 pound bananas (about 2 large)
¼ cup Apricot Glaze (page 66)
¼ cup chopped pistachio nuts (optional)
1-2 teaspoons rum (optional)

1. Put the tart shell on the serving plate. Spread the pastry cream on the tart shell.

2. Peel and slice the bananas into ⅛-inch segments.

3. Arrange the slices on the pastry cream, starting at the outside edge and working toward the center, overlapping slightly (diagram 6, page 75).

4. Brush the bananas with a little glaze. Sprinkle on the nuts. Spritz with rum.

5. Serve within 2 hours.

VARIATIONS
Instead of the Flaky Pastry Tart Shell try:
Whole Wheat Flaky Pastry Tart Shell (page 41)
Nut Pastry Tart Shell (page 44)
Chocolate Nut Pastry Tart Shell (page 45)
Meringue (page 45), Nut Meringue (page 46) or Cocoa Meringue (page 46)
    Tart Shell (assemble only at the last minute)

Instead of Classic Pastry Cream try:
Praline Pastry Cream (page 60)
Nut Pastry Cream (page 44)
Chocolate Pastry Cream (page 46)
Alcoholic Pastry Cream (page 53)
Alcoholic Pastry Cream (page 53) with Grand Marnier (omit rum spritz)

....

BLACKBERRY TART

1 pound blackberries (about 1 pint)
Baked Flaky Pastry Tart Shell (page 40)
½ cup Classic Pastry Cream (page 52) or any plain pastry cream
¼ cup Raspberry Glaze (page 69)
1-2 teaspoons kirschwasser or Grand Marnier (optional)

1. If the blackberries seem dirty or dusty, rinse and drain them; otherwise do not.

2. Put the tart shell on the serving plate. Spread the pastry cream on the tart shell.

3. Arrange the blackberries on the pastry cream, stem side down, starting at the outside edge and working toward the center. Pack the berries together as tightly as possible without crushing them.

4. Brush with a little glaze. Spritz on kirschwasser or Grand Marnier.

5. Serve within 2 hours.

VARIATIONS
Instead of the Flaky Pastry Tart Shell try:
Whole Wheat Flaky Pastry Tart Shell (page 41)
Nut Pastry Tart Shell (page 44)
Cinnamon Nut Pastry Tart Shell (page 45)
Classic Puff Pastry Tart Shell (page 38)
Sweet Pastry Tart Shell (page 42)
Meringue (page 45) or Nut Meringue (page 46) Tart Shell (assemble only
   at the last minute)

Instead of Classic Pastry Cream try:
Nut Pastry Cream (page 54)
Alcoholic Pastry Cream (page 53) with brandy
Spice Pastry Cream (page 54)
Or omit pastry cream. Brush the tart shell with a little glaze and sprinkle ¼ cup Crushed Almond Macaroon Filling (page 59) on the glaze before arranging the berries.

BOYSENBERRY TART

1 pound boysenberries (about 1 pint)
Baked Flaky Pastry Tart Shell (page 40)
½ cup Classic Pastry Cream (page 52) or any plain pastry cream
¼ cup Raspberry Glaze (page 69)
1-2 teaspoons kirschwasser or Grand Marnier (optional)

1. If the boysenberries are dusty or dirty, rinse them; otherwise do not.

2. Put the tart shell on the serving plate. Spread the pastry cream on the tart shell.

3. Arrange the boysenberries on the pastry cream, stem side down, starting at the outside edge and working toward the center. Pack the berries together as tightly as possible without crushing them.

4. Brush with a little glaze. Spritz on kirschwasser or Grand Marnier.

5. Serve within 2 hours.

VARIATIONS
Instead of the Flaky Pastry Tart Shell try:
Whole Wheat Flaky Pastry Tart Shell (page 41)
Nut Pastry Tart Shell (page 44)
Cinnamon Nut Pastry Tart Shell (page 45)
Classic Puff Pastry Tart Shell (page 38)
Sweet Pastry Tart Shell (page 42)
Meringue (page 45) or Nut Meringue (page 46) Tart Shell (assemble
   only at the last minute)

Instead of Classic Pastry Cream try:
Nut Pastry Cream (page 54)
Alcoholic Pastry Cream (page 53) with Grand Marnier
Or omit pastry cream. Brush the tart shell with a little glaze and
   sprinkle ¼ cup Crushed Almond Macaroon Filling (page 59) on the
   glaze before arranging the berries.

CHERRY TART

1½ pounds fresh Bing cherries
Baked Flaky Pastry Tart Shell (page 40)
¼ cup Raspberry Glaze (page 69)
¼ cup Crushed Almond Macaroon Filling (page 59)
1-2 teaspoons kirschwasser or brandy (optional)

1. Preheat the oven to 400°F.

2. Stem, wash and pit the cherries. Put on a baking sheet lined with waxed or parchment paper and bake about 5 minutes, until the juices start to be released. Cool.

3. Put the tart shell on the serving plate. Brush the bottom of the tart shell with a little glaze and sprinkle the crushed macaroons on the glaze.

4. Arrange the cherries on the macaroons, starting at the outside edge and working toward the center. Pack the cherries together as tightly as possible, concealing the pit shafts.

5. Brush with a little glaze. Spritz on kirschwasser or brandy.

6. Serve within 3 hours.

VARIATIONS
Instead of the Flaky Pastry Tart Shell try:
Sweet Pastry Tart Shell (page 42)
Nut Pastry Tart Shell (page 44)
Meringue (page 45) or Nut Meringue (page 46) Tart Shell (assemble only at the last minute)

Instead of Raspberry Glaze try:
Chocolate Glaze (page 66)

BRANDIED CHERRY TART

You can brandy your own cherries, as explained below, or purchase them at a quality food shop.

1 pound brandied cherries
Baked Flaky Pastry Tart Shell (page 40)
¼ cup Raspberry Glaze (page 69)
¼ cup Crushed Almond Macaroon Filling (page 59)

1. Drain and pit the cherries.

2. Put the tart shell on the serving plate. Brush the tart shell with a little glaze. Sprinkle the crushed macaroons on the glaze.

3. Arrange the cherries on the macaroons, starting at the outside edge and working toward the center. Pack them together as tightly as possible, concealing the pit shafts.

4. Brush the cherries with a little glaze.

5. Serve within 3 hours.

BRANDIED CHERRIES
1 pound fresh Bing cherries
Brandy to cover

1. Sterilize a sealable jar (see page 63).

2. Stem and rinse the cherries. Put them in the sterilized jar and cover with brandy. Seal the jar and let the cherries steep in a cool place away from light for about a month, or until they sink in the liquid.

3. If the cherries are not to be used within a week after they sink, drain the brandy. Cover the cherries with a syrup made by boiling 3 cups each water and sugar. Seal and store in a cool place away from light.

VARIATIONS
Instead of the Flaky Pastry Tart Shell try:
Sweet Pastry Tart Shell (page 42)
Whole Wheat Flaky Pastry Tart Shell (page 41)
Nut Pastry Tart Shell (page 44)

Meringue (page 45) or Nut Meringue (page 46) Tart Shell (assemble only at the last minute)

Instead of Raspberry Glaze try:
Chocolate Glaze (page 66)

CHERRY TART WITH HOLLANDAISE

Baked Flaky Pastry Tart Shell (page 40)
1 pound fresh Bing cherries (canned unsweetened cherries are acceptable)
Hollandaise Pastry Filling (page 56), at room temperature
1–2 teaspoons kirschwasser or brandy (optional)
Powdered sugar

1. Preheat the oven to 350°F.

2. Leave the tart shell in the tart tin and put it on a baking sheet.

3. Stem, wash and pit the cherries, or drain the canned cherries.

4. Spread a ¼-inch layer of hollandaise on the tart shell. Press all but ¼ cup of the cherries into the hollandaise. Spread the remaining hollandaise on the cherries. Level the top with a palette knife.

5. Bake about 25–30 minutes, until golden brown. Immediately release the tart to a cooling rack.

6. Spritz on the kirschwasser or brandy. Sprinkle with powdered sugar and arrange the remaining cherries on the tart.

7. Serve within 10 hours.

CHERRY AND LEMON CUSTARD TART

½ pound fresh Bing cherries (canned unsweetened cherries are acceptable)
Baked Flaky Pastry Tart Shell (page 40)
Lemon Custard (page 57)

1. Preheat the oven to 400°F.

2. Stem, wash and pit the cherries, or drain the canned cherries.

3. Leave the tart shell in the tart tin and put it on a baking sheet.

4. Lay the cherries in the tart shell. Spread the custard over the cherries.

5. Bake about 20–25 minutes, until dark brown spots appear on top.

6. Release the tart to a cooling rack.

7. Serve within 10 hours.

COCONUT TART

Baked Flaky Pastry Tart Shell (page 40)
Frangipane (page 58)
1 cup unsweetened grated coconut (3 ounces)
2–3 tablespoons Apricot Glaze (page 66) or lemon marmalade
2–3 tablespoons rum (optional)

1. Preheat the oven to 350°F.

2. Leave the tart shell in the tart tin.

3. Mix the frangipane with the coconut. Brush the glaze or marmalade over the tart shell and spread the frangipane-coconut mixture over the glaze.

4. Bake about 25–30 minutes, until golden brown. Release from the tart tin to a cooling rack.

5. Spritz with rum.

6. Serve within 10 hours.

CRANBERRY TART

Baked Flaky Pastry Tart Shell (page 40)
1 pound cranberries (about 1 pint)
⅓ cup Raspberry Glaze (page 69)
Hollandaise Pastry Filling (page 56), at room temperature
1-2 teaspoons Grand Marnier (optional)
Powdered sugar

1. Preheat the oven to 350°F.

2. Leave the tart shell in the tart tin and put it on a baking sheet.

3. In a heavy saucepan, poach the cranberries in the glaze about 5 minutes, or until the berries begin to pop. Cool and drain off the excess glaze.

4. Spread a ¼-inch layer of hollandaise on top of the tart shell. Press all but ½ cup of the berries into the hollandaise. Spread the remaining hollandaise on the berries.

5. Bake about 25–30 minutes, until golden brown. Remove from the oven and immediately release the tart to a cooling rack.

6. When completely cooled, spritz on the Grand Marnier. Sprinkle with powdered sugar and place the remaining berries on top as a garnish.

7. Serve within 10 hours.

Note. You can also poach the cranberries in Apricot (page 66) or Peach (page 68) Glaze instead of Raspberry Glaze.

CURRANT TART

1 pound currants (about 1 pint)
¼ cup Raspberry Glaze (page 69)
Baked Flaky Pastry Tart Shell (page 40)
½ cup Classic Pastry Cream (page 52) or any plain pastry cream
1-2 teaspoons kirschwasser (optional)

1. Rinse and stem the currants. Put them in a bowl with the glaze. Stir until glaze coats every berry. Drain off excess glaze.

2. Put the tart shell on the serving plate. Spread the pastry cream on the tart shell.

3. Spoon the currants over the pastry cream.

4. Spritz with kirschwasser.

5. Serve within 6 hours.

VARIATIONS
Instead of the Flaky Pastry Tart Shell try:
Classic Puff Pastry Tart Shell (page 38)
Nut Pastry Tart Shell (page 44)

CURRANT AND RASPBERRY TART

6 ounces currants (about ½ pint)
¼ cup Raspberry Glaze (page 69)
6 ounces raspberries (about ½ pint)
Baked Flaky Pastry Tart Shell (page 40)
½ cup Classic Pastry Cream (page 52) or any plain pastry cream
1-2 teaspoons kirschwasser (optional)

1. Rinse the currants. Put them in a bowl with the glaze and stir until the glaze coats each currant. Drain off the excess glaze (reserve it to brush on the raspberries).

2. If the raspberries are dusty or dirty, rinse them; otherwise do not.

3. Put the tart shell on the serving plate. Spread the pastry cream on the tart shell.

4. Arrange the berries and currants in alternating rings, starting at the outside edge and working toward the center.

5. Brush the raspberries with a little glaze. Spritz on kirschwasser.

6. Serve within 3 hours.

VARIATIONS
Instead of the Flaky Pastry Tart Shell try:
Nut Pastry Tart Shell (page 44)
Sweet Cinnamon Pastry Tart Shell (page 43)

Instead of Classic Pastry Cream try:
Nut Pastry Cream (page 54)
Spice Pastry Cream (page 54)

DATE TART

The dates should be marinated for at least 24 hours before the tart is assembled.

1 pound dates
¼ cup brandy (2 ounces)
Baked Flaky Pastry Tart Shell (page 40)
¼ cup Apricot Glaze (page 66)
¼ cup Crushed Almond Macaroon Filling (page 59)
24 whole blanched almonds

1. Pit the dates and steep them in the brandy for at least 24 hours in a covered container. Drain.

2. Put the tart shell on the serving plate. Brush the tart shell with a little glaze. Sprinkle the crushed macaroons on the glaze.

3. Arrange the dates on the macaroons. Pack the dates together as tightly as possible, concealing the pit shafts. Arrange the almonds on the dates.

4. Brush with a little glaze.

5. Serve within 5 hours.

DRIED FRUIT TART

Dried fruit should be marinated for at least three days, so plan ahead if you want to make this tart.

1 cup sugar
1 cup water
1 lemon or orange rind, peeled off with a potato peeler
⅓ cup brandy
1 pound dried fruit (apricots, figs, dates, raisins, prunes)
Baked Flaky Pastry Tart Shell (page 40)
¼ cup Apricot Glaze (page 66)
¼ cup Crushed Almond Macaroon Filling (page 59)
24 whole almonds or walnuts

1. Put the sugar, water and rind in a heavy saucepan. Cook at a full boil for 2 minutes. Cool and add the brandy. Pour over the fruit. Cover securely and steep for at least three days (up to four or five months) at room temperature.

2. Drain the fruit.

3. Put the tart shell on the serving plate. Brush the bottom of the tart shell with a little glaze. Sprinkle the crushed macaroons on the glaze.

4. Arrange the fruit on the crushed macaroons, starting at the outside edge and working toward the center, overlapping slightly. Arrange the nuts on the fruit.

5. Brush with a little glaze.

6. Serve within 5 hours.

FIG TART

1 pound figs (about 12 small)
Baked Flaky Pastry Tart Shell (page 40)
½ cup Classic Pastry Cream (page 52) or any plain pastry cream
¼ cup Strawberry Glaze (page 70)
1-2 teaspoons Grand Marnier or brandy (optional)

1. Wash and dry the figs and cut off the pip ends.

2. Put the tart shell on the serving plate. Spread the pastry cream on the tart shell.

Method 1

3. Split the figs into half along the length. Arrange the halves, cut side up, on the pastry cream, starting at the outside edge (diagram 4, page 74). Continue with Step 4.

Method 2

3. Quarter the figs by slicing the halves along the length. Arrange these wedges, cut side up, starting at the outside edge in a row radiating toward the center. Arrange the next row in the ring, and fill in the center with another radiating row (diagram 1, page 74).

4. Brush the figs with a little glaze. Spritz on the Grand Marnier or brandy.

5. Serve within 4 hours.

VARIATIONS
Instead of the Flaky Pastry Tart Shell try:
Nut Pastry Tart Shell (page 44)
Nut Meringue Tart Shell (page 46) (assemble only at the last minute)

....

GRAPE TART

1 pound purple or green grapes, preferably seedless
Baked Flaky Pastry Tart Shell (page 40)
½ cup Classic Pastry Cream (page 52) or any plain pastry cream
¼ cup Apricot Glaze (page 66)
1-2 teaspoons Grand Marnier (optional)

1. Rinse and stem the grapes. If the grapes are not seedless, cut them in half and remove the seeds.

2. Put the tart shell on the serving plate. Spread the pastry cream on the tart shell.

Method 1

3. Arrange the whole grapes, stem side down, on the pastry cream, starting at the outside edge and working toward the center. Pack them together as tightly as possible. Continue with Step 4.

Method 2

3. Arrange the grape halves, starting at the outside edge and working toward the center, overlapping slightly in a camellia pattern (diagram 7, page 75).

4. Brush with a little glaze. Spritz on the Grand Marnier.

5. Serve within 3 hours.

VARIATIONS
Instead of the Flaky Pastry Tart Shell try:
Nut Pastry Tart Shell (page 44)
Sweet Pastry Tart Shell (page 42)
Meringue (page 45) or Nut Meringue (page 46) Tart Shell (assemble only
   at the last minute)

GRAPEFRUIT TART

Oranges or tangerines can be substituted for the grapefruit segments.

¾ pound grapefruit segments (from about 4 grapefruit; see step 1)
Baked Flaky Pastry Tart Shell (page 40)
½ cup Classic Pastry Cream (page 52) or any plain pastry cream
¼ cup Citrus Glaze (page 67)

1. To prepare the grapefruit, peel away the rind and the inner white skin. (A serrated knife works better than a straight-edged blade.) Do not be afraid of wasting some of the flesh; better to waste a little than end up with some of the bitter inner skin. Make two cuts through to the center of the fruit on either side of the inner skin that separates the segments and pull out each segment.

2. Lay the segments on a towel to drain.

3. Put the tart shell on the serving plate and spread the pastry cream on it.

4. Arrange the grapefruit segments on the pastry cream, starting at the outside edge and working toward the center, overlapping slightly in a camellia pattern (diagram 7, page 75).

5. Brush with a little glaze.

6. Serve within 2 hours.

KIWI TART

The kiwi fruit of New Zealand looks like a brown furry egg on the outside, but on the inside it is a beautiful lime green with black spots at the core. Somewhat tart, it has a flavor reminiscent of strawberries. Buy kiwi fruit that are slightly soft, like a ripe peach.

Baked Flaky Pastry Tart Shell (page 40)
½ cup Classic Pastry Cream (page 52) or any plain pastry cream
¾ pound kiwi fruit (about 3 large)
¼ cup Apricot Glaze (page 66)
1-2 teaspoons kirschwasser or Grand Marnier (optional)

1. Put the tart shell on the serving plate. Spread the pastry cream on the tart shell.

2. Peel the kiwi fruit with straight-bladed knife.

Method 1

3. Slice the kiwi fruit into ⅛-inch segments across the width. Discard the end piece with the pip.

4. Arrange the slices on the pastry cream, starting at the outside edge and working toward the center, overlapping slightly (diagram 6, page 75). Continue with Step 5.

Method 2

3. Cut the pip end off the kiwi fruit; cut the kiwi in half along the length and then in quarters and eighths along the length.

4. Arrange these wedges in a row radiating toward the center, starting at the outside edge, rounded side down. Arrange another row in a ring, and fill in the center with another radiating row (diagram 1, page 74).

5. Brush with a little glaze. Spritz on kirschwasser or Grand Marnier.

6. Serve within 2 hours.

VARIATIONS

Instead of the Flaky Pastry Tart Shell try:

Nut Pastry Tart Shell (page 44)

Classic Puff Pastry Tart Shell (page 38)

Whole Wheat Flaky Pastry Tart Shell (page 41)

Meringue (page 45), Nut Meringue (page 46) or Cocoa Meringue (page 46) Tart Shell (assemble only at the last minute)

Instead of Classic Pastry Cream try:

Nut Pastry Cream (page 54)

Alcoholic Pastry Cream (page 53) with Grand Marnier

Praline Pastry Cream (page 53)

KUMQUAT TART

At least a month's marinating time is required for the kumquats so plan ahead.

2 cups sugar
2 cups water
⅔ cup brandy
½ pound kumquats
Baked Flaky Pastry Tart Shell (page 40)
Lemon Custard (page 57)

1. In a heavy saucepan, boil the sugar and water for 1 minute.

2. Remove from the heat and add the brandy.

3. Sterilize a sealable jar (see page 63). Wash the kumquats; pour boiling water over them and drain. Put the kumquats in the still-hot jar and pour the hot syrup over them. Seal and store in a cool place away from light for at least a month.

4. Preheat the oven to 400°F.

5. Leave the tart shell in the tart tin and put it on a baking sheet.

6. Drain the syrup off the kumquats. Cut each kumquat in half and remove the seeds. Lay the kumquats in the tart shell.

7. Spread the lemon custard over the kumquats.

8. Bake about 20–25 minutes, or until dark brown spots appear on top.

9. Release the tart to a cooling rack.

10. Serve within 10 hours.

LEMON CUSTARD TART

Baked Flaky Pastry Tart Shell (page 40)
2–3 tablespoons lime marmalade
Lemon Custard (page 57)

1. Preheat the oven to 400°F.

2. Leave the tart shell in the tart tin and put it on a baking sheet.

3. Spread the marmalade on the tart shell. Pour the custard over the marmalade and level it with a palette knife.

4. Bake about 20 minutes, until very dark spots appear on the custard. (Rotate the tart in the oven if necessary to prevent one side from becoming too dark.) Immediately release the tart to a cooling rack.

5. Serve within 10 hours.

VARIATIONS
Instead of Lemon Custard try:
Lime Custard (page 57)
Orange Custard (page 57)
Chocolate Glaze (page 66)

··

LOQUAT TART

The loquat, a member of the citrus family, looks like a yellow cherry and grows wild on the California coast. Not much flesh surrounds the large stone, but it is sweet, succulent and delicious.

3 pounds loquats
1 cup sugar
3 tablespoons grated lemon rind
Unbaked Nut Pastry Tart Shell (page 44)

1. Rinse and pit the loquats. Measure 1 cup. Put the loquats, sugar and lemon rind in a heavy saucepan and stir until the sugar is dissolved.

2. Bring to a full boil while stirring, being careful that the mixture does not boil over. Turn the heat down to a low boil and cook about 20–25 minutes, until a spoonful of the mixture becomes set or jellylike after 5 minutes in the refrigerator.

3. Skim off the foam.

4. Preheat the oven to 350°F.

5. Put the tart tin on a baking sheet and pour the loquat mixture into the tart shell.

6. Bake about 25–30 minutes, until the tart shell is slightly brown and the loquats seem set.

7. Immediately release the tart to a cooling rack.

8. Serve within 10 hours.

MANDARIN ORANGE TART

¾ pound mandarin orange segments (from about 5 mandarin oranges)
Baked Flaky Pastry Tart Shell (page 40)
½ cup Classic Pastry Cream (page 52) or any plain pastry cream
¼ cup Citrus Glaze (page 67)

1. To prepare the mandarin oranges, peel away the rind and the white inner skin. (A serrated knife blade works better than a straight-edged blade.) Do not be afraid of wasting some of the flesh; better to waste a little than end up with some of the bitter inner skin. Make two cuts through to the center of the fruit on either side of the inner skin that separates the segments and pull out each segment.

2. Put the segments on a towel to drain.

3. Put the tart shell on the serving plate. Spread the pastry cream on the tart shell.

4. Arrange the mandarin orange segments on the pastry cream, starting at the outside edge and working toward the center, overlapping slightly in a camellia pattern (diagram 7, page 75).

5. Brush with a little glaze.

6. Serve within 2 hours.

VARIATIONS
Instead of the Flaky Pastry Tart Shell try:
Nut Pastry Tart Shell (page 44)
Sweet Pastry Tart Shell (page 42)
Classic Puff Pastry Tart Shell (page 38)
Meringue (page 45), Nut Meringue (page 46) or Cocoa Meringue (page 46) Tart Shell (assemble only at the last minute)

Instead of Classic Pastry Cream try:
Praline Pastry Cream (page 53)
Nut Pastry Cream (page 54)

MANGO TART

1 pound mangoes (about 2 medium)
Baked Flaky Pastry Tart Shell (page 40)
½ cup Classic Pastry Cream (page 52) or any plain pastry cream
¼ cup Apricot Glaze (page 66)
1-2 teaspoons rum or Grand Marnier (optional)

1. Peel the mangoes. Lay them flat and score lines ⅛ inch apart through to the pit along the length. Liberate the slices from the pit by one stroke of the knife, scraping the edge of the pit.

2. Put the tart shell on the serving plate. Spread the pastry cream on the tart shell.

3. Arrange the mango slices on the pastry cream, starting at the outside edge and working toward the center, overlapping slightly in a camellia pattern (diagram 7, page 75).

4. Brush with a little glaze. Spritz with rum or Grand Marnier.

5. Serve within 2 hours.

VARIATIONS
Instead of the Flaky Pastry Tart Shell try:
Coconut Pastry Tart Shell (page 47)
Nut Pastry Tart Shell (page 44)
Sweet Pastry Tart Shell (page 42)
Sweet Cinnamon Pastry Tart Shell (page 43)

Instead of Classic Pastry Cream try:
Praline Pastry Cream (page 53)
Nut Pastry Cream (page 54)
Spice Pastry Cream (page 54)

NECTARINE TART

The nectarines can be prepared up to two days in advance.

1 pound slightly underripe nectarines (2 large or 3 small)
2 cups water
2 cups sugar (part peach or strawberry glaze or jelly if desired)
1 orange rind, peeled off with a potato peeler
1-inch piece cinnamon stick
5 whole cloves
Baked Flaky Pastry Tart Shell (page 40)
½ cup Classic Pastry Cream (page 52) or any plain pastry cream
¼ cup Strawberry Glaze (page 70)
¼ cup chopped pistachio nuts (optional)
1–2 teaspoons brandy (optional)

1. Wash, halve and pit the nectarines (do not peel them; less of the flavor will be leached out). In a heavy saucepan, bring the water and sugar to a boil. Turn down the heat to a simmer and add the rind and spices. Add the nectarines. Cover and poach about 20 minutes, until they are soft but still sliceable.

2. Drain on a rack. Do not rub off the skin. Cover and store in the refrigerator. (Reserve the liquid for future use. Cover securely and store in the refrigerator.)

3. Put the tart shell on the serving plate. Spread the pastry cream on the tart shell.

4. Gently rub the skin off the nectarines.

Method 1

5. Lay the nectarine halves flat and slice into ⅛-inch segments across the width. Arrange the nectarine slices on the pastry cream, starting at the outside edge and working toward the center, overlapping slightly in a camellia pattern (diagram 7, page 75). Continue with Step 6.

. . . .

Method 2

5. Reserve one nectarine half and score a lattice pattern halfway through it. Lay the remaining nectarine halves flat and slice them into ⅛-inch segments across the width. Put the scored half in the center of the tart shell and arrange the slices to radiate from it, overlapping slightly (diagram 5, page 75). Continue with Step 6.

Method 3

5. Score a lattice pattern halfway through the nectarine halves. Arrange them on the tart shell (diagram 4, page 74). Continue with Step 6.

Method 4

5. Lay the nectarine halves flat and slice them into ⅛-inch segments across the width. Slide a palette knife underneath each half and press the slices until they fan out slightly. Keeping all the slices on the palette knife, transfer them to the tart shell, gently sliding them off onto the pastry cream (diagram 6, page 75).

6. Brush with a little glaze. Sprinkle on the nuts. Spritz on brandy.

7. Serve within 2 hours.

VARIATIONS

Instead of the Flaky Pastry Tart Shell try:
Nut Pastry Tart Shell (page 44)
Cinnamon Nut Pastry Tart Shell (page 45)

Instead of Classic Pastry Cream try:
Alcoholic Pastry Cream (page 53) with brandy
Nut Pastry Cream (page 54)

OLALLIEBERRY TART

In appearance very similar to blackberries, olallieberries have a flavor between raspberry and blackberry.

1 pound olallieberries (about 1 pint)
Baked Flaky Pastry Tart Shell (page 40)
½ cup Classic Pastry Cream (page 52) or any plain pastry cream
¼ cup Raspberry Glaze (page 69)
1-2 teaspoons kirschwasser or Grand Marnier (optional)

1. If the olallieberries are dusty or dirty, rinse them; otherwise do not.

2. Put the tart shell on the serving plate. Spread the pastry cream on the tart shell.

3. Arrange the berries, stem side down, on the pastry cream, starting at the outside edge and working toward the center. Pack the berries together as tightly as possible without crushing them.

4. Brush with a little glaze. Spritz on kirschwasser or Grand Marnier.

5. Serve within 2 hours.

VARIATIONS
Instead of the Flaky Pastry Tart Shell try:
Nut Pastry Tart Shell (page 44)
Classic Puff Pastry Tart Shell (page 38)
Sweet Pastry Tart Shell (page 42)
Meringue (page 45), Nut Meringue (page 46) or Cocoa Meringue (page 46) Tart Shell (assemble only at the last minute)

Instead of Classic Pastry Cream try:
Praline Pastry Cream (page 53)
Nut Pastry Cream (page 54)
Spice Pastry Cream (page 54)
Alcoholic Pastry Cream (page 53) with Grand Marnier
Or omit pastry cream. Brush the tart shell with a little glaze and sprinkle on ¼ cup Crushed Almond Macaroon Filling (page 59) before arranging the berries.

....

PAPAYA TART

1 pound papayas (about 2 large)
Baked Flaky Pastry Tart Shell (page 40)
½ cup Classic Pastry Cream (page 52) or any plain pastry cream
¼ cup Apricot Glaze (page 66)
1–2 teaspoons rum or Grand Marnier (optional)

1. Peel and halve the papayas. Scoop out the seeds. Lay the halves flat and slice into ⅛-inch segments across the width.

2. Put the tart shell on the serving plate. Spread the pastry cream on the tart shell.

3. Arrange the papaya slices on the pastry cream, starting at the outside edge and working toward the center, overlapping slightly in a camellia pattern (diagram 7, page 75).

4. Brush with a little glaze. Spritz on rum or Grand Marnier.

5. Serve within 2 hours.

VARIATIONS
Instead of the Flaky Pastry Tart Shell try:
Coconut Pastry Tart Shell (page 47)
Nut Pastry Tart Shell (page 44)
Sweet Pastry Tart Shell (page 42)
Sweet Cinnamon Pastry Tart Shell (page 43)
Meringue (page 45), Nut Meringue (page 46) or Cocoa Meringue (page 46)
   Tart Shell (assemble only at the last minute)

Instead of Classic Pastry Cream try:
Praline Pastry Cream (page 53)
Nut Pastry Cream (page 54)
Spice Pastry Cream (page 54)

....

PEACH AND RASPBERRY TART MELBA

½ pound poached peaches (see page 112 for poaching instructions)
½ pound raspberries (½ pint)
Baked Flaky Pastry Tart Shell (page 40)
½ cup Classic Pastry Cream (page 52) or any plain pastry cream
¼ cup Strawberry Glaze (page 170)
24 blanched almonds
1–2 teaspoons kirschwasser (optional)

1. Lay the peaches on a towel to drain away the excess moisture. Gently rub off the skin. Lay the peaches flat and slice into ⅛-inch segments across the width.

2. If the raspberries are dusty or dirty, rinse them; otherwise do not.

3. Put the tart shell on the serving plate. Spread the pastry cream on the tart shell.

4. Arrange the two different fruits in alternating rings, starting at the outside edge and working toward the center.

5. Brush with a little glaze. Arrange the almonds on the fruit. Spritz on kirschwasser.

6. Serve within 2 hours.

VARIATIONS
Instead of the Flaky Pastry Tart Shell try:
Classic Puff Pastry Tart Shell (page 38)
Nut Pastry Tart Shell (page 44)
Nut Meringue Tart Shell (page 46) (assemble only at the last minute)

Instead of Classic Pastry Cream try:
Nut Pastry Cream (page 54)

··

PEACH TART

The peaches can be poached and stored in the refrigerator up to two days in advance.

1 pound slightly underripe peaches (2 large or 3 small)
2 cups water
2 cups sugar (part peach or strawberry glaze or jelly if desired)
1 lemon rind, peeled off with a potato peeler
1-inch piece cinnamon stick
5 whole cloves
Baked Flaky Pastry Tart Shell (page 40)
½ cup Classic Pastry Cream (page 52) or any plain pastry cream
¼ cup Strawberry Glaze (page 70)
¼ cup chopped pistachio nuts (optional)
1–2 teaspoons brandy (optional)

1. Wash, halve and pit the peaches (do not peel; less of the flavor will be leached out).

2. In a heavy saucepan, bring the water and sugar to a boil. Turn down the heat to a simmer and add the rind and spices. Add the peaches. Cover and poach about 20 minutes, until they are soft but still sliceable.

3. Drain on a rack. Do not rub off the skin. Cover and store in the refrigerator until ready to use. (Reserve the liquid for future use. Cover securely and store in the refrigerator.)

4. Put the tart shell on the serving plate. Spread the pastry cream on the tart shell. Gently rub the skin off the peaches.

Method 1

5. Lay the peach halves flat and slice into ⅛-inch segments across the width. Arrange the peach slices on the pastry cream, starting at the outside edge and working toward the center, overlapping slightly in a camellia pattern (diagram 7, page 75). Continue with Step 6.

··

Method 2

5. Reserve one peach half and score a lattice pattern halfway through it. Lay the remaining peach halves flat and slice them into ⅛-inch segments across the width. Put the scored half in the center of the tart shell and arrange the slices to radiate from it, overlapping slightly (diagram 5, page 75). Continue with Step 6.

Method 3

5. Score a lattice pattern halfway through the peach halves. Arrange them on the tart shell (diagram 2, page 74). Continue with Step 6.

Method 4

5. Lay the peach halves flat and slice them into ⅛-inch segments across the width. Slide a palette knife underneath each half and press the slices until they fan out slightly. Keeping all the slices on the palette knife, transfer them to the tart shell, gently sliding them off onto the pastry cream (diagram 3, page 74).

6. Brush with a little glaze. Sprinkle on the nuts. Spritz with brandy.

7. Serve within 2 hours.

VARIATIONS
Instead of the Flaky Pastry Tart Shell try:
Nut Pastry Tart Shell (page 44)
Cinnamon Nut Pastry Tart Shell (page 45)
Classic Puff Pastry Tart Shell (page 38)

Instead of Classic Pastry Cream try:
Alcoholic Pastry Cream (page 53) with brandy
Nut Pastry Cream (page 54)

D'anjou pear sauce firmer : poach better

BURGUNDY PEAR TART

This tart is perhaps the most beautiful of them all and, as one friend complimented me, as good as anything on this earth can be. The Burgundy pears can be prepared and stored in the refrigerator up to two days in advance.

1 pound slightly underripe D'Anjou pears (2 large or 3 small)
3 cups Burgundy (Zinfandel is also delicious)
1 cup sugar
1 vanilla bean (optional)
Baked Flaky Pastry Tart Shell (page 40)
½ cup Classic Pastry Cream (page 52) or any plain pastry cream
¼ cup Raspberry Glaze (page 69)
¼ cup chopped pistachio nuts (optional)

1. Peel, halve and core the pears.

2. In a heavy saucepan, bring the wine, sugar and vanilla bean to a boil. Turn down to a simmer and add the pears. Cover and poach about 20 minutes, until soft but still sliceable.

3. Drain and cool on a rack. Cover and refrigerate. (Reserve the liquid for future use. Cover and store in the refrigerator.)

4. Put the tart shell on the serving plate. Spread the pastry cream on the tart shell. Lay the pears flat and slice them into ⅛-inch segments across the width. Drain on a towel.

Method 1

5. If using 3 small pears, slide a palette knife underneath each sliced half and gently press the slices until they fan out slightly. Keeping all the slices on the palette knife, transfer them to the tart shell, gently sliding them off onto the pastry cream (diagram 3, page 74). Continue with Step 6.

Method 2

5. If using only 2 pears, arrange the slices starting at the outside edge and working toward the center, overlapping slightly in a camellia pattern (diagram 7, page 75).

6. Brush with a little glaze. Sprinkle on the chopped nuts.

7. Serve within 2 hours.

VARIATIONS
Instead of the Flaky Pastry Tart Shell try:
Nut Pastry Tart Shell (page 44)
Classic Puff Pastry Tart Shell (page 38)

··

SPICED PEAR TART

The pears can be prepared and stored in the refrigerator up to two days in advance.

1 pound slightly underripe D'Anjou pears
2 cups water
2 cups sugar
1 lemon rind, peeled off with a potato peeler
1 cinnamon stick
5 whole cloves
Baked Flaky Pastry Tart Shell (page 40)
½ cup Classic Pastry Cream (page 52)
¼ cup Apricot Glaze (page 66)
¼ cup sliced almonds (optional)

1. Peel, halve and core the pears.

2. In a heavy saucepan bring the water, sugar, rind and spices to a boil. Turn down to a simmer and add the pears. Cover and poach about 20 minutes until soft but still sliceable.

3. Drain and cool on a rack. Cover and store in the refrigerator. (Reserve the liquid for future use. Cover and store in the refrigerator.)

4. Follow the procedure for making the Burgundy Pear Tart (page 114).

PERSIMMON TART

1 pound persimmons (2 large or 3 small)
Baked Flaky Pastry Tart Shell (page 40)
½ cup Classic Pastry Cream (page 52) or any plain pastry cream
¼ cup Apricot Glaze (page 66)
¼ cup chopped pistachio nuts (optional)
1–2 teaspoons kirschwasser or Grand Marnier (optional)

1. Peel the persimmons and slice into ⅛-inch segments across the width. Discard the end slice with the pip.

2. Put the tart shell on the serving plate. Spread the pastry cream on the tart shell.

3. Arrange the persimmon slices on the pastry cream, starting at the outside edge and working toward the center, overlapping slightly (diagram 6, page 75).

4. Brush with a little glaze. Sprinkle on the nuts. Spritz on kirschwasser or Grand Marnier.

5. Serve within 2 hours.

VARIATIONS
Instead of the Flaky Pastry Tart Shell try:
Classic Puff Pastry Tart Shell (page 38)
Nut Pastry Tart Shell (page 44)
Cinnamon Nut Pastry Tart Shell (page 45)
Nut Meringue Tart Shell (page 46) (assemble only at the last minute)

Instead of Classic Pastry Cream try:
Nut Pastry Cream (page 54)
Spice Pastry Cream (page 54)

PINEAPPLE TART

One 2-pound ripe pineapple
Baked Flaky Pastry Tart Shell (page 40)
½ cup Classic Pastry Cream (page 52) or any plain pastry cream
¼ cup Citrus Glaze (page 67)
¼ cup chopped pistachio nuts (optional)
1–2 teaspoons rum or Grand Marnier (optional)

1. With a sharp cleaver or chef's knife, peel, quarter and eighth the pineapple. Lay each eighth flat and slice into ⅛-inch segments. Trim away the pulpy center part and remove any remaining eyes with the tip of a potato peeler. Split the segments again if they are thicker than ¼ inch.

2. Drain on a towel.

3. Put the tart shell on the serving plate. Spread the pastry cream on the tart shell.

4. Arrange the pineapple slices on the pastry cream, starting at the outside edge and working toward the center, overlapping slightly in a camellia pattern (diagram 7, page 75).

5. Brush with a little glaze. Sprinkle on the chopped pistachio nuts. Spritz on rum or Grand Marnier.

6. Serve within 2 hours.

VARIATIONS
Instead of the Flaky Pastry Tart Shell try:
Classic Puff Pastry Tart Shell (page 38)
Nut Pastry Tart Shell (page 44)
Meringue (page 45), Nut Meringue (page 46) or Cocoa Meringue (page 46) Tart Shell (assemble only at the last minute)

Instead of Classic Pastry Cream try:
Nut Pastry Cream (page 54)
Alcoholic Pastry Cream (page 53) with rum or Grand Marnier

PLUM TART

1 pound ripe plums
Baked Flaky Pastry Tart Shell (page 40)
½ cup Classic Pastry Cream (page 52) or any plain pastry cream
¼ cup Strawberry Glaze (page 70)

1. Halve and pit the plums. Lay them flat and slice into ⅛-inch segments along the length.

2. Put the tart shell on the serving plate. Spread the pastry cream on the tart shell.

3. Arrange the plum slices on the pastry cream, starting at the outside edge and working toward the center, overlapping slightly in a camellia pattern (diagram 7, page 75).

4. Brush with a little glaze.

5. Serve within 4 hours.

VARIATIONS
Instead of the Flaky Pastry Tart Shell try:
Whole Wheat Flaky Pastry Tart Shell (page 41)
Nut Pastry Tart Shell (page 44)
Sweet Pastry Tart Shell (page 42)

BAKED ITALIAN PLUM TART

Baked Flaky Pastry Tart Shell (page 40)
1 pound prune or Italian plums (10 small)
Custard for Cooked Tarts (page 58) (omit nuts)
½ cup Plum Glaze (page 68)

1. Preheat the oven to 350°F.

2. Leave the tart shell in the tart tin and put it on a baking sheet.

3. Wash and dry the plums, halve along the length, and pit.

Method 1

4. Arrange the plum halves, pit side up, in a row radiating toward the center from the outside edge. Arrange another row in a ring and fill in the center with another radiating row (diagram 4, page 74). Continue with Step 5.

Method 2

4. Slice the plums into eighths along the length. Starting at the outside edge, arrange the segments in a row radiating toward the center and overlapping slightly. Arrange another row of segments inside the first row, going in the opposite direction—if the first row radiated clockwise, the second row should radiate counterclockwise (diagram 1, page 74).

5. Pour the custard around the plums and brush a little glaze on the plums.

6. Bake 15 minutes. Remove from the oven and brush a little more glaze on the plums. Return to the oven and bake about another 15 minutes, or until the edges of the plums start to get brown and the custard turns a golden brown. Immediately release the tart to a cooling rack.

7. Brush the entire tart (not just the plums) with glaze.

8. Serve within 6 hours.

···

QUINCE TART

The quinces can be poached and refrigerated up to two days in advance.

1 cup sugar
2 cups water
¼ cup lemon marmalade (or other flavorful jelly or jam)
¼ cup brandy
¾ pound quinces (about 2 large for Method 1, 3–4 small for other methods)
Baked Flaky Pastry Tart Shell (page 40)
½ cup Classic Pastry Cream (page 52) or any plain pastry cream
¼ cup Strawberry Glaze (page 70)
¼ cup chopped walnuts or almonds (optional)
1–2 tablespoons brandy (optional)

1. Bring the sugar, water and marmalade to a boil in a heavy saucepan. Turn the heat down to a low boil and add the brandy.

2. Peel, halve and core the quinces. Poach, covered, about 20 minutes, until soft yet still sliceable.

3. Drain on a rack and cool. Cover and refrigerate. (Reserve the liquid for future use. Cover and store in the refrigerator.)

4. Put the tart shell on the serving plate. Spread the pastry cream on the tart shell.

Method 1

5. Lay the quince halves flat and slice them into ⅛-inch segments across the width. Arrange the quince slices on the pastry cream, starting at the outside edge and working toward the center, overlapping slightly in a camellia pattern (diagram 1, page 74). Continue with Step 6.

Method 2

5. Reserve one quince half and score a lattice pattern halfway through it. Lay the remaining quince halves flat and slice them into ⅛-inch segments across the width. Put the scored half in the center of the tart shell and arrange the slices to radiate from it, overlapping slightly (diagram 5, page 75). Continue with Step 6.

Method 3

5. Score a lattice pattern halfway through the quince halves. Arrange the quince halves in the tart shell (diagram 2, page 74). Continue with Step 6.

Method 4

5. Lay the quince halves flat and slice them into ⅛-inch segments across the width. Slide a palette knife underneath each half and press the slices until they fan out slightly. Keeping all the slices on the palette knife, transfer them to the tart shell, gently sliding them off onto the pastry cream (diagram 3, page 74).

6. Brush with a little glaze. Sprinkle on the nuts. Spritz on brandy.

7. Serve within 2 hours.

RHUBARB TART

Baked Flaky Pastry Tart Shell (page 40)
1 pound rhubarb
Custard for Cooked Tarts (page 58) (omit nuts)
¼ cup Raspberry Glaze (page 69)

1. Preheat the oven to 350°F.

2. Leave the tart shell in the tart tin and put it on a baking sheet.

3. Wash the rhubarb and remove the strings. Slice into ⅛-inch segments. Lay the rhubarb segments in the tart shell and pour the custard over them.

4. Bake about 25–30 minutes, or until the custard turns a golden brown. Immediately release the tart to a cooling rack.

5. Brush the entire surface with a little glaze.

6. Serve within 6 hours.

RHUBARB AND APPLE TART

Baked Flaky Pastry Tart Shell (page 40)
½ pound apples (about 1 large or 2 small)
½ pound rhubarb
½ cup Strawberry Glaze (page 70) or jam

1. Preheat the oven to 350°F.

2. Leave the tart shell in the tart tin and put it on a baking sheet.

3. Peel, halve, core and grate the apples. Measure 1 cup.

4. Rinse the rhubarb, pull the strings off and slice into ⅛-inch segments.

5. Mix the apples, rhubarb and glaze or jam. Pour into the tart shell and level with a spatula.

6. Bake about 25 minutes, or until the filling seems set.

7. Immediately release from the tart tin to a cooling rack.

8. Serve within 10 hours.

RASPBERRY TART

Baked Flaky Pastry Tart Shell (page 40)
Frangipane (page 58)
1 pound raspberries (about 1 pint)
¼ cup Raspberry Glaze (page 69)
1–2 teaspoons kirschwasser (optional)

1. Preheat the oven to 350°F.

2. Leave the tart shell in the tart tin. Spread the frangipane on the tart shell. Put on a baking sheet and bake about 20–25 minutes, until golden brown. Cool thoroughly.

3. If the raspberries are dusty or dirty, rinse and drain them; otherwise do not.

4. Put the tart shell on the serving plate.

5. Arrange the raspberries, stem side down, on the frangipane, starting at the outside edge and working toward the center. Pack together as tightly as possible without crushing them.

6. Brush with a little glaze. Spritz on kirschwasser.

7. Serve within 6 hours.

VARIATIONS
Instead of the Flaky Pastry Tart Shell try:
Classic Puff Pastry Tart Shell (page 38) (use with a pastry cream instead of the frangipane filling)
Nut Pastry Tart Shell (page 44) (use with a pastry cream instead of the frangipane filling)
Sweet Pastry Tart Shell (page 42)
Meringue (page 45) or Nut Meringue (page 46) Tart Shell (use with a pastry cream instead of the frangipane filling and assemble only at the last minute)

Instead of the frangipane filling try:
Classic Pastry Cream (page 52) or any plain pastry cream
Or omit pastry cream and brush the tart shell with a little glaze. Sprinkle on ¼ cup Crushed Almond Macaroon Filling (page 59) before arranging the berries.

STRAWBERRY TART

1 pound strawberries (about 1 pint)
Baked Flaky Pastry Tart Shell (page 40)
½ cup Classic Pastry Cream (page 52) or any plain pastry cream
¼ cup Strawberry Glaze (page 70)
1-2 teaspoons kirschwasser (optional)

1. Rinse and stem the berries.

2. Put the tart shell on the serving plate. Spread the pastry cream on the tart shell.

Method 1

3. Arrange the whole strawberries on the pastry cream, starting at the outside edge and working toward the center. Pack them together as tightly as possible without crushing them. Continue with Step 4.

Method 2

3. Cut the berries in half from the point down, reserving one perfect whole berry for the center. Arrange the berries, pointing outward, starting at the outside edge and working toward the center, overlapping slightly. Put the whole berry in the center. Continue with Step 4.

Method 3

3. Cut the berries in half from the point down, reserving one perfect berry for the center. Put the whole berry in the center and lean the half berries against it. Continue in concentric rings until the entire tart is covered. (This method works well with very large berries.)

4. Brush with a little glaze. Spritz on kirschwasser.

5. Serve within 2 hours.

VARIATIONS
Instead of the Flaky Pastry Tart Shell try:
Nut Pastry Tart Shell (page 44)
Sweet Pastry Tart Shell (page 42)
Classic Puff Pastry Tart Shell (page 38)
Chocolate Pastry Tart Shell (page 46)
Chocolate Nut Pastry Tart Shell (page 45)
Meringue (page 45), Nut Meringue (page 46) or Cocoa Meringue (page
    46) Tart Shell (assemble only at the last minute)

Instead of Classic Pastry Cream try:
Praline Pastry Cream (page 53)
Alcoholic Pastry Cream (page 53) with kirschwasser
Nut Pastry Cream (page 54)
Or omit pastry cream and bake the tart shell with Frangipane (page 58)

DIETER'S TART

*There are only 100–120 calories per serving of this tart. Strawberries are
low in calories.*

¾ pound strawberries (about ¾ pint)
Meringue Tart Shell (page 45)
½ cup Pastry Cream Made with Yogurt (page 54)
1 tablespoon Strawberry Glaze (page 70)

1. Wash and stem the strawberries.

2. Put the tart shell on the serving plate. Spread the pastry cream on the
tart shell.

3. Arrange the strawberries on the tart as in the Strawberry Tart (page
126).

4. Brush with the glaze.

5. Serve within 1 hour.

RED, WHITE AND BLUE FRUIT TART

To celebrate the Fourth of July or Bastille Day.

½ pound blueberries (about ½ pint)
¼ cup Raspberry Glaze (page 69)
½ pound strawberries or raspberries (about ½ pint)
Baked Flaky Pastry Tart Shell (page 40)
½ cup Classic Pastry Cream (page 52) or any plain pastry cream
¼ cup Strawberry (page 70) or Raspberry Glaze (page 69)
½ cup heavy cream
1 tablespoon sugar
1 teaspoon kirschwasser (optional)

1. In a heavy saucepan, poach the blueberries in ¼ cup raspberry glaze for about 5 minutes, until they begin to pop. Drain and cool.

2. Rinse and stem the strawberries or raspberries. If the raspberries are dusty or dirty, rinse them; otherwise do not.

3. Put the tart shell on the serving plate. Spread the pastry cream on the tart shell.

4. Arrange the red berries and the blueberries in alternating rings, starting at the outside edge and working toward the center.

5. Brush the strawberries or raspberries with a little glaze.

6. At serving time, whip the cream with the sugar and kirschwasser. Dollop the cream on top of each serving, or use a pastry bag to pipe out the cream in a decorative way.

7. Spritz on additional kirschwasser.

8. Serve within 2 hours.

VARIATIONS
Instead of the Flaky Pastry Tart Shell try:
Classic Puff Pastry Tart Shell (page 38)
Nut Pastry Tart Shell (page 44)
Sweet Pastry Tart Shell (page 42)

CHRISTMAS TART

Green kiwi fruit and red strawberries make a colorful holiday tart.

6 ounces kiwi fruit (2 small)
½ pound strawberries (½ pint)
Baked Flaky Pastry Tart Shell (page 40)
½ cup Classic Pastry Cream (page 52) or any plain pastry cream
2 tablespoons Apricot Glaze (page 66)
2 tablespoons Strawberry Glaze (page 70)
1-2 teaspoons kirschwasser (optional)

1. Peel the kiwi fruit and slice into ⅛-inch segments across the width.

2. Rinse and stem the strawberries. Cut them in half if they are very large.

3. Put the tart shell on the serving plate. Spread the pastry cream on the tart shell.

4. Arrange the two different fruits in alternating rings, starting at the outside edge and working toward the center.

5. Brush the kiwi fruit with the apricot glaze and the strawberries with the strawberry glaze. Spritz on kirschwasser.

6. Serve within 2 hours.

VARIATIONS
Instead of the Flaky Pastry Tart Shell try:
Classic Puff Pastry Tart Shell (page 38)
Sweet Pastry Tart Shell (page 42)
Nut Pastry Tart Shell (page 44)
Meringue (page 45) or Nut Meringue (page 46) Tart Shell (assemble only at the last minute)

Instead of Classic Pastry Cream try:
Nut Pastry Cream (page 54)

BERRY-BERRY TART

Red raspberries contrast beautifully with blackberries. A combination of berries produces a depth of flavor without being unclassical.

1 pound mixed berries (blackberries, boysenberries, olallieberries, raspberries)
Baked Flaky Pastry Tart Shell (page 40)
½ cup Classic Pastry Cream (page 52) or any plain pastry cream
¼ cup Raspberry Glaze (page 69)
1-2 teaspoons kirschwasser (optional)

1. If the berries are dusty or dirty, rinse them; otherwise do not.

2. Put the tart shell on the serving plate. Spread the pastry cream on the tart shell.

3. Arrange the different berries in alternating rings, starting at the outside edge and working toward the center. Pack them together as tightly as possible without crushing them.

4. Brush with a little glaze. Spritz on kirschwasser.

5. Serve within 2 hours.

VARIATIONS
Instead of the Flaky Pastry Tart Shell try:
Nut Pastry Tart Shell (page 44)
Cinnamon Nut Pastry Tart Shell (page 45)
Sweet Pastry Tart Shell (page 42)
Meringue (page 45), Nut Meringue (page 46) or Cocoa Meringue (page 46) Tart Shell (assemble only at the last minute)

Instead of Classic Pastry Cream try:
Nut Pastry Cream (page 54)
Alcoholic Pastry Cream (page 53) with Grand Marnier or kirschwasser
Or omit pastry cream. Brush the bottom of the tart shell with a little glaze. Sprinkle Crushed Almond Macaroon Filling (page 59) on the glaze before arranging the berries.

used papaya, banana, + kiwi

TARTE TROPICALE

½ pound pineapple slices
1 kiwi fruit
1 mango
Baked Flaky Pastry Tart Shell (page 40)
½ cup Classic Pastry Cream (page 52) or any plain pastry cream
¼ cup Apricot Glaze (page 66)
¼ cup coarsely chopped macadamia nuts (1 ounce)
1–2 tablespoons rum (optional)

1. Prepare the pineapple as in steps 1 and 2 of the Pineapple Tart (page 118).

2. Peel and slice the kiwi fruit into ⅛-inch segments across the width.

3. Prepare the mango as in step 1 of the Mango Tart (page 106).

4. Put the tart shell on the serving plate. Spread the pastry cream on the tart shell.

5. Arrange the different fruits in alternating rings, starting at the outside edge and working toward the center, overlapping slightly.

6. Brush with a little glaze. Sprinkle on the nuts. Spritz on rum.

7. Serve within 3 hours.

VARIATIONS
Instead of the Flaky Pastry Tart Shell try:
Coconut Pastry Tart Shell (page 47)
Nut Pastry Tart Shell (page 44)

Instead of Plain Pastry Cream try:
Alcoholic Pastry Cream (page 53) with rum
Nut Pastry Cream (page 54)
Spice Pastry Cream (page 54)

MIXED CITRUS FRUIT TART

¾ pound mixed citrus fruit segments (About 4 different fruits—such as
   orange, mandarin orange, grapefruit, and tangerine)
Baked Flaky Pastry Tart Shell (page 40)
½ cup Classic Pastry Cream (page 52) or any plain pastry cream
¼ cup Citrus Glaze (page 67)

Follow the procedure for the Grapefruit Tart (page 99).

MAIL ORDER GUIDE

Bazaar Français of the Market, Inc.
668 Sixth Avenue
New York, NY 10010
Equipment only, excellent selection

Bissinger's
205 West 4th Street
Cincinnati, OH 45202
Equipment

Istanbul Express
2432 Durant Avenue
Berkeley, CA 94704
Excellent selection of chocolate

Lekvar by the Barrel
H. Roth and Son
1577 First Avenue
New York, NY 10028
*Excellent selection of equipment and
ingredients, including flour and
vanilla beans*

Maid of Scandinavia
3244 Raleigh Avenue
Minneapolis, MN 55416
*Equipment and ingredients, includ-
ing chocolate and vanilla beans*

Paprikas Weiss Importer
1546 Second Avenue
New York, NY 10028
*Ingredients, including vanilla beans,
and some equipment*

Williams-Sonoma Mail Order
   Department
P.O. Box 3792
San Francisco, CA 94119
*Excellent selection of equipment and
some ingredients*

INDEX